by Murray Soupcoff
and Gary Dunford

with Rick Salutin

James Lorimer & Company, Publishers

Toronto 1975

ISBN 0-88862-089-6   paper

Photos courtesy of: Public Archives of Canada
                     Miller Services
                     Information Canada
                     Canadian Press

James Lorimer & Company, Publishers
35 Britain Street
Toronto

Printed and bound in Canada

Canadian Shared Cataloguing in Publication Data

Soupcoff, Murray.
   Good buy, Canada!

ISBN 0-88862-089-6 pbk.

1.Canadian wit and humor. 2. Canada —
Civilization — Anecdotes, facetiae, satire,
etc. I. Dunford, Gary. II. Salutin, Rick.
III. Title.

PN6178.C3S68   817'.5'4

The All-Canadian Believe This or Not!
✶✶✶✶ ✶ 100% Canadian Content

PIERRE JUNEAU CHAIRMAN OF THE CANADIAN RADIO-TELEVISION COMMISSION HAS <u>NEVER</u> SEEN OR HEARD A RADIO OR TELEVISION PROGRAM !!! SUBMITTED BY JOHN BASSETT, TORONTO.

THE ALBERTA OIL SANDS ARE NOT REALLY SANDS AT ALL AND THERE IS NO OIL IN THEM. AND WE'RE RAISING THE PRICE OF OIL FOUR CENTS A GALLON NEXT WEEK !!!

— CANADA'S OIL COMPANIES
(WE CAN HARDLY BELIEVE IT!)

THE JARVIS STREET TRIANGLE

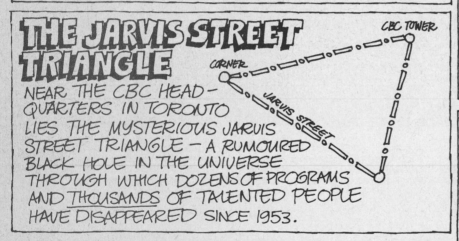

NEAR THE CBC HEADQUARTERS IN TORONTO LIES THE MYSTERIOUS JARVIS STREET TRIANGLE — A RUMOURED BLACK HOLE IN THE UNIVERSE THROUGH WHICH DOZENS OF PROGRAMS AND <u>THOUSANDS</u> OF TALENTED PEOPLE HAVE DISAPPEARED SINCE 1953.

RON BASFORD'S BALD SPOT CAN BE SEEN UP TO 500 MILES AWAY ON A CLEAR NIGHT. IF IT'S NOT RON YOU SPOT, THEN IT MUST HAVE BEEN THE REFRACTED GLOW FROM TELLY SAVALAS IN NEW YORK !!!

WAYNE AND SHUSTER... ARE ONE AND THE SAME PERSON. IT IS NOT CLEAR HOW OR WHY, BUT HOW COME WE ALWAYS HAVE TROUBLE REMEMBERING WHICH ONE IS WHICH? FOR FURTHER DETAILS WRITE TO WAYNE AND/OR SHUSTER AT THE CBC....

POTATO IN THE SHAPE OF **JULIETTE, 62 POUNDS.** GROWN BY WILBUR BOONEY, PRINCE EDWARD ISLAND.

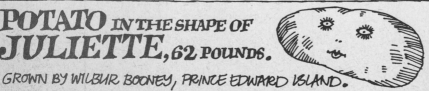

FOR RENT...

LOVABLE T.V. FAMILY. SLIGHTLY USED, BUT EASILY RESTORED TO FORMER GRANDEUR. ANTIQUE STORY LINE NOW COMPLETELY RENOVATED. WAS RENTING FOR $50,000 A WEEK. NOW AVAILABLE FOR $25 AN INSTALMENT. GREAT CONVERSATION PIECE FOR WEDDINGS AND SWEET SIXTEENS. THIS MONTH ONLY, COMES COMPLETE WITH FLASHBACKS AND THREE PREMATURELY-RETIRED CBC EXECUTIVES. A STEAL AT ANY PRICE. WRITE TO «DISASTER», WHITEOAKS OF JALNA, BOX 25, CBC, TORONTO

ALL ABOUT BOOKS
BY GUESS WHO

Inside-from-the-Outside's **GOOD BUY, CANADA** by Soupcoff, Dunford & Salutin James Lorimer and Co., ~~$4.95~~ $5.95

It was a quiet, cold night when this pulp volume arrived at my home and, as is usually my wont, I took it to the living room to settle before the fire for a pleasant evening's entertainment.

With a cookie and a hot milk, and lowering the lights, I began with the title page — which as usual is found at the front of the book — and with long, lingering movements, began tearing the pages from top to bottom in smooth, uninterrupted strips.

Lighting the first few strips with an Eddy match, I soon found the pages casting a cozy glow about the room, each page of this marvellous volume catching quickly and burning with a good blue flame for maximum heat.

The fireplace crackled and snapped, the sweet smell of fresh, burning newsprint everywhere, and I thought I caught a glimpse of several familiar faces (continued on page 589)...

6 steps to the most unreliable mail service anywhere.

We're out to make Canada's postal system the worst in the world. And believe it or not, we don't have far to go. We've introduced some sophisticated new processing equipment that is bound to increase employee discontent and ensure even more work stoppages and negligence. And now there are six things you can do (if you're not already doing them) to get even worse service. Help us to cripple Canada's postal system. Not just for a strike, or a walkout . . . but for good.

MEMO TO STAFF
Are we meeting the Postal Standards? If so, where are we going wrong? Please advise.

Circulate to:

_____ _____
(Name)   (Initial)

_____ _____

_____ _____

_____ _____

Please return unread to:

_____
(Signed)

1 Don't write your return address in this space. In fact, don't write it anywhere. Then if there's any problem, we can throw the letter away. (If you have been writing your return address in this space, don't worry. We throw the letter away anyway.)

2 This is the last place to put your postage. Try inside the envelope instead. Then when we're rifling through, looking for money or credit cards, we can lift the stamp too.

3 The address can be written or typed in any part of 3 & 4, but don't pay much attention to the accuracy of street, city, or postal code. We don't.

4 The Postal Code must appear as the last item on the address. That way we can really be sure to ignore it. If you want, try making up your own postal codes. Your letter will still only take three months to get to any city in Canada.

5 Please leave this space — 18mm (¼ in.) — entirely blank (so our sorters can doodle on it while they work to rule).

6 Don't bother sealing your envelope. It's only going to get unsealed from our rough handling. (Besides we'll probably lose your letter anyway, and you'll have done all that licking for nothing.)

P. E. Trudeau
24 Sussex Drive
Ottawa, Ontario   K1A 0B3

Canada 3

PERSONAL & CONFIDENTIAL

Postmaster General
Parliament Buildings
OTTAWA, Ontario
K1A 2R5

…e have m…
…oor handling of…
…pear to be unfit a…
…e your resignation a…
…no longer employ you as Pos…

…core to…
…incompete…
…much regre…

The envelope is as important to us as the letter is to you.

Postal   Canada
Canada   Postale

These basic guidelines apply to envelopes measuring less than 1600 mm x 1800 mm (13 ft. x 14 ft.). All other envelopes must be shipped by truck.

For further information telegraph: Postal Standards, Ottawa, Ontario K1A 0Y2
Don't write. The letter will probably get lost on the way.

Christmas and New Year's Cards from Famous Canadians

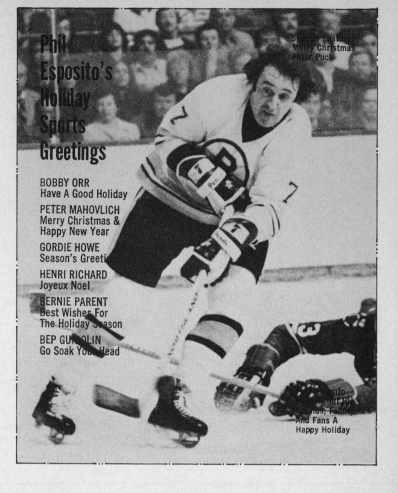

Phil Esposito's Holiday Sports Greetings

Special Feature
Merry Christmas
Peter Puck

BOBBY ORR
Have A Good Holiday

PETER MAHOVLICH
Merry Christmas &
Happy New Year

GORDIE HOWE
Season's Greeti...

HENRI RICHARD
Joyeux Noel

BERNIE PARENT
Best Wishes For
The Holiday Season

BEP GUIDOLIN
Go Soak Your Head

Esposito...
...All His
...ends, Family
And Fans A
Happy Holiday

Cut them out and fool your friends

REPORT ON GORDON SINCLAIR'S BUSINESS

Gordon Sinclair ends year with Merry Christmas and Happy New Year

Prices of almost all Gordon Sinclair's stocks rose at the end of a year of mixed trading for the well-known broadcaster and financier. In addition, revenues from broadcasting and television appearances increased in value for the fifth straight year.

Overall volume was down 11 per cent, but Mr. Sinclair blames the decline on the sluggish Canadian economy and his reduced work schedule.

Among the bigger gains for Mr. Sinclair were increased revenue from "Front Page Challenge" and a new multi-year contract with Toronto radio station CFRB.

Losses included a bet that the Dow Jones Industrial Index would reach the 1000 point mark again, and speculation in non-fluoridated water commodities.

Mr. Sinclair looks forward to a merry Christmas and a happy and prosperous New Year, and wishes the same good cheer for all his family, friends and colleagues.

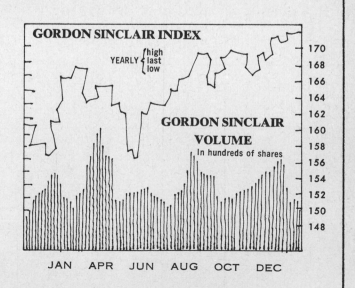

GORDON SINCLAIR INDEX

YEARLY { high
last
low

170
168
166
164
162
160
158
156
154
152
150
148

GORDON SINCLAIR VOLUME
In hundreds of shares

JAN   APR   JUN   AUG   OCT   DEC

Have a Happy New Year

By MME JEHANE BENOIT

New Year's has always been a time of good cheer, so why not forget the overwhelming social and economic problems that weigh on the shoulders of all of us. Forget rising prices, higher interest charges on your car, larger mortgage payments on your house, even the increasing costs of sending your children to university . . . . Well, try and forget them, by following the following recipe for having a happy New Year.

CELEBRATING NEW YEAR'S

There's nothing like a New Year's Eve drunk to make everything seem rosy again. Just remember, an ounce of moderation on New Year's Eve avoids a splitting headache and queasy stomach on New Year's morning.

1 bottle scotch
1 bottle rye
1 bottle vodka
1 bottle ginger ale
1 bottle Aspirin
1 bottle Alka Seltzer

Pour four parts scotch in glass. Add 1 part water. Stir and add ice to taste. Drink.

Mix 3 parts rye with one part ginger ale. Allow to fizz. Add ice and drink.

Fill two glasses with vodka and drink. And drink. And drink.

Prepare Aspirins and Alka Seltzer for next morning.

Recline on chair or couch.

Your troubles are over, for this evening anyway.

JULIETTTE'S SCHEDULE FOR DEC. 25th*

MON., DEC. 24 TO FRI., JAN. 1

SEASON'S GREETINGS FROM JULIETTE

morn

8:00 Sleep In — Better Health
Having completed another hectic week of television and radio appearances, Juliette takes advantage of the Christmas morning holiday to oversleep.

9:00 Wake Up — Light Drama
Roused by the kids next door playing with their new G.I. Joe bazooka, Juliette gets up and finds several gifts under the Christmas tree.

9:30 Open Gifts — Variety
Juliette opens her Christmas gifts, including a new G.E. dishwasher, a Volvo station wagon and a year's subscription to Ms. Magazine.

10:00 Breakfast — Cooking

After driving her new station wagon into the kitchen, Juliette sits down to a traditional Christmas breakfast of buttered toast, marmalade and hot Metrecal.

10.30 Call Mom — Nostalgia
Juliette calls Mom and wishes her a Merry Christmas. Other songs include "Silent Night," "O Little Town of Bethlehem" and "Rudolph The Red-Nosed Reindeer".

11:00 Visitors — Interview
The personable CBC television starlet welcomes her Christmas guests, including the Allen Sisters, Tommy Banks and Lloyd Robertson. Juliette joins with her guests in wishing all of her family, friends and fans a happy yuletide holiday.

*Listings in Juliette's Christmas schedule are based on the latest information from Canada's most famous starlet. However, Juliette has often been known to make last-minute changes in her yuletide activities. For this information, please consult Juliette or her publicity agent between 9 and 5 PM weekdays.

National bestsellers

This National Bestseller list is compiled by an exhaustive survey of all bookstores within a 1300 feet radius of our nearest tavern.

1. The Last Cookie,
   (Volume Two of Air Canada History) by Pierre Berton   1   6
2. You Can Survive An Economic Depression,
   by E. P. Taylor   4   25
3. The Royalty Cheque That Wouldn't Float,
   by Farley Mowat with Jack McClelland   2   47
4. My Ten Favourite Final Issues of "Saturday
   Night" Magazine, by Robert Fulford   10   20
5. He Signs, He Cashes His Cheque! The Story
   Of Hockey In The 70's, by Brian McFarfle   —   22
6. The New Canadian Bible, by Howie Meeker   4   8
7. How To Lose A Million, by Johnny Bassett Jr.   8   14
8. Read Canadian — Special Two And A Half
   Page Edition, by Mordecai Richler   3   22
9. My Twelve Most Unforgettable Mars Bars
   Commercials, by Nancy Greene   11   45
10. The Candy Factory And Other Foreign Takeovers,
    by Laura Secord as told to Fanny Farmer   16   3

THE UNITED STATES

1976 and All That Stuff

To insure distribution of this book in the United States, Federal Law requires us to insert a token U.S. section of news. This is it. It is written by the Inside-from-the-Outside Washington bureau (a 16-year-old kid we hired from the Peoria Bulletin-Star on a dare).

Since 1946, when Peter 'Columbo' Falk discovered America and the New World, the panoply of Western man has rolled downhill towards this very week: the U.S. Quinto-Centennial.

Accordingly, this week in the nation's capital, Los Angeles, President Edgar Ford touched off a year of celebration as he lit the Centennial flame.

Prominent Americans attending the event were Willy Brandt, Harold Wilson and Merv Griffin.

In another part of the city, Secretary of Defence Otto Preminger dedicated a monument to famous American frontiersman and cooking magnate, Davey Crocker.

Although other nations were represented, Canada declined to send a representative since it was the day of Otto Lang's birthday.

When told of Canada's action, President Ford furrowed his brow and told this reporter:

(PICK UP WIRE SERVICE COPY)

and walked away in disgust.

Elsewhere, reaction ranged from

(SEE NEW YORK TIMES MONDAY)

to

(MAKE IT UP TO FILL UP THE PARAGRAPH)

President Ford

another week of historic hoopla in the diary of the Republic.

The Magic Majority
A Story in Words and Pictures
for the Children of Canada

This is
a majority

This is the
Philosopher King

This is
his house

This is
unemployment

What ???
A $1·50 for
butter ?

This is
inflation

This is the story of the

and the magic

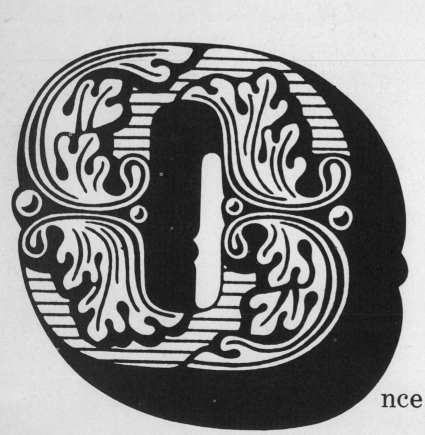 nce upon a time,

there was a  He lived in a big

And he ruled over the Kingdom of

from  to  But the Kingdom

of 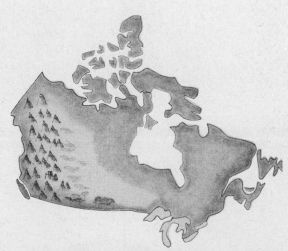 was not happy.

There was too much

And too much

And of course
too much control of

by

 o the

said to his advisors. "How can I make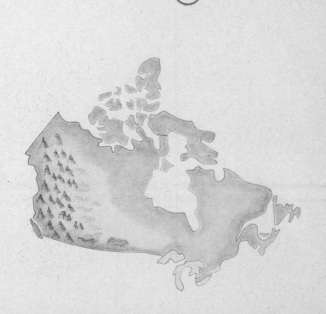

and of course the control of

by  disappear? I've tried

I've tried  I've tried

I've even tried consulting

But none of these ills will go away."

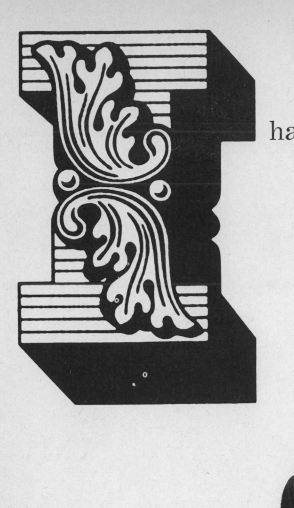have a solution,"

 told the

"What you need is something magic. A

that will make all your problems disappear."

o the

left his  and

travelled through  looking for

the magic  On his way,

 he met and

who were also looking for a

But  and didn't have

And so the

soon belonged to the and he brought it back to the

he  was happy.

Now  and

and the control of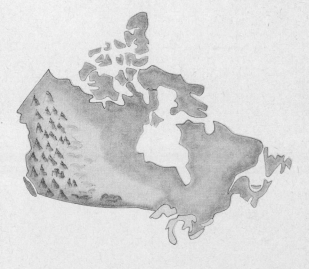

by  would disappear.

But weeks passed. Then months passed.
And none of these ills went away. In fact, they got worse.

o one, however,
was brave enough

to tell the

 wouldn't tell him.

 wouldn't tell him.

Even 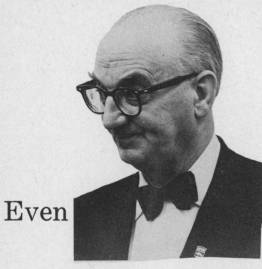 wouldn't tell him.

They didn't want the  to be angry with them.

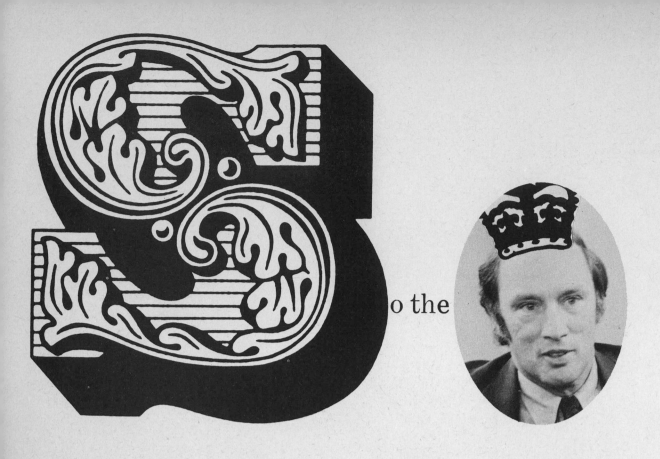o the

was happy with his magic

happy that finally the universe was unfolding as it should.

But the Kingdom of  got worse and worse and worse.

There was more  more

and even more control of

by All the while the

went on happily reassuring
the people of

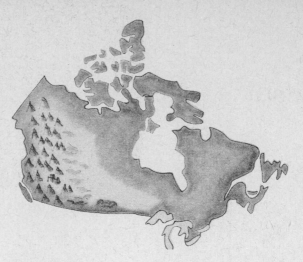

that they never had it so good.

hen one day,

a bright little boy,

came into the  And he saw that

 and his advisors
were deceiving themselves.

That the

was not magic and that the universe was indeed not
unfolding as it should. And so bravely he summoned up
all his courage and shouted as loud as he could :

"Hurrah for the  !"

Why? Because this is a real story, not a fairytale. And in reality, the only way the little boy was going

to become  himself was to go along

with the present  Which he did.

Until it was too late.

And the kingdom of

lived unhappily ever after. *The End*

NO TURNEZ LA PAGE!

VIOLATION

BILINGUALISM AND BICULTURALISM COMMISSION

Vous have comitted un serieux and grave offence against la Queen, les langues Canadiennes and Keith Spicer. Vous must not turnez la page if the sign says No Turnez La Page!

OFFENCE 417-2AF-16

SEEN BY Sgt. W. Voyeur

Bilingualism/Biculturalism
Strategic Attack Force, Unit #22

LOCATION Page **29**
Inside from the Outside Book

DESCRIPTION Subject did wilfully and maliciously turn page contrary to International No Turnez La Page Sign.

PUNISHMENT:
- ☐ Four weeks in Intensive Immersion French Course with 16 Bored G-14 Civil Servants
- ☐ A bilingual date with Keith Spicer
- ☐ Writing "No Turnez la Page" 1,000 times with figure skates on the floor of the Montreal Forum
- ☐ Jean Marchand's old portfolios

DATE 2/16/76

Return this card with your payment and choice of punishment to the Commission Deux Tongues et Tetes, Ottawa K1Y 2E6.

MODERN GADGETRY HELPS KEEP OUR STREETS FREE OF CRIME

— AN EXCLUSIVE I.F.T.O. PHOTO REPORT —

Proud members of New York's finest try out the latest addition to their crime-fighting equipment, the MR-100 Anti-Pickpocket Vehicle. The fully-mechanized unit fires a powerful salvo at suspected pickpockets, immediately immobilizing them until police can make an arrest. There have been some problems with wounded bystanders and damaged storefronts, but police expect to have those wrinkles ironed out in a few months.

Catching speeders has always been a problem for Quebec's Provincial Police. However, all that's past now as Corporal Gilles Lafleur demonstrates, with the QPP's latest weapon against speeding, the C-120 police fighter plane. Gilles makes a warning dive over a speeding vehicle, and if the driver still doesn't get the message, a burst of machine gun fire across his windshield usually gets the desired result.

Anti-littering laws on Halifax's waterfront are there for a purpose — to keep the harbour clean. But until recently, the laws didn't seem to carry the proper authority — until, that is, harbour police purchased the new Horning-Douglas 16-gun patrol boat pictured above. Now harbour police are able to pick up any sign of littering on the boat's sensitive radar and rush to the scene of the crime. Police say that since they instituted regular patrols by the Horning-Douglas, littering has dropped nearly 60%.

What do you do when a gang of black militants have holed up in a tenement building and refuse to give themselves up? Los Angeles police have come up with the solution — blast them out with the new Wessun-Jones Anti-Black-Militants Gun.

If there are hostages, it can get a little messy, but at least law-abiding citizens can sleep at night, secure in the knowledge that their city is once again safe from ghetto violence and lawlessness.

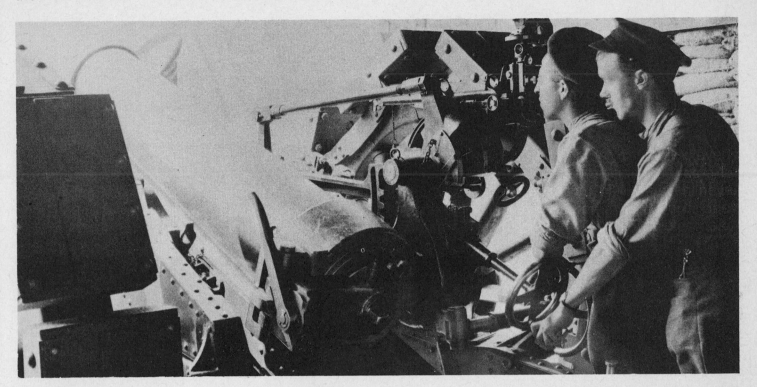

When milk-store robberies in Winnipeg began to increase at an alarming rate recently, police took immediate action. Noting that the robberies seemed to follow a pattern in the city's core, they fed their information to a computer and asked it to predict the site of the next robbery. The computer obliged and eight of Winnipeg's finest cleverly set up a camouflaged ambush for the would-be robbers (see picture above). The thieves never arrived, but had they ventured into that area, they would have received a very explosive welcome.

In the opinion of many Vancouver residents, the use of drugs and marijuana at teen-age parties has gotten out of hand. Vancouver police have responded to this grave situation and, borrowing from the very latest urban tactical battle plans, have made a series of lightning raids on teen-age pot and glue-sniffing parties.

Members of the RCMP have been complaining lately about the ineffectiveness of their bullets. What with all the protective clothing and bulletproof vests worn by modern-day criminals, the Mounties just haven't been getting their man. So in response to their pleas, their crime laboratory has been manufacturing larger more explosive bullets, as pictured above, guaranteed to cut down the toughest criminals. The Mounties' problem now is to invent a revolver big enough to hold the new bullets.

Finally, Hamilton police have once again demonstrated to the criminal element that it doesn't pay to break the law. Suspected drug dealer Manuel Wolinsky was arrested on drug charges in a pre-dawn raid on his luxurious midtown home. However, despite a tip from a reliable informer, police were unable to find the cache of drugs they were looking for. They suspected that the suspect had flushed the incriminating evidence down a drain, but couldn't be sure. In the past, they would have meekly withdrawn, but now equipped with amazing new Walden One-Step Homewrecker (see picture), they tore down Wolinsky's home piece by piece in their search for the incriminating evidence. Unfortunately, they couldn't find it, but it will be a warning to other wrongdoers not to trifle with the law.

The Immigration Game...

🍁 Immigration Canada

PORT OF ENTRY INTERVIEW FORM FOR POTENTIAL LANDED IMMIGRANT

Warning: DO NOT SHOW THIS FORM TO APPLICANT OR THE GLOBE AND MAIL BY ORDER OF THE MINISTER

POINT TOTAL MUST EQUAL AT LEAST 60 OF POSSIBLE 100 FOR ENTRY.

Ricco Nixxon   _4/6/76_   _H. Hardy_

Name of applicant   Date   Name of Interviewing Officer
(no points for knowing name)   (25 points for knowing name)

Nice Man

National Origin
Orangeman (10 points)
United States (10 points)
Europeans (except Wops) (8 points)
Wops (2 points, 3½ if hard worker)
Chinks (no points, unless railroad under construction)
Polacks (1 point; 15 if agree in writing to settle in Newfoundland)
Pakistani, West Indian and other riffraff (are you kidding?)

Appearance of applicant
_____ Trendy (10 points)
_____ Jeans (minus 10)
_____ Boutique jeans w/appliqué (7 points)
__X__ Busines suit and external affairs briefcase (20 points)
_____ John Turner hairsyle or other Dry Look (5 points)
_____ Gay (minus 2)
_____ Racist lecturer (5 points)

DO NOT WRITE IN THIS SPACE

Why the hell not?

Race, which we are not allowed to ask
The Canadian Government abides by all dictums of the Human Rights Act and would never think of asking the racial background of an applicant. Ha ha. What colour are you? __X__ White (10 points) Black (1 point for trying) _____ Red (none) _____ Albino (2) _____ Paisley Print ($3.99 a yard)

Friends of Minister
Met minister at
_____ party
_____ embassy function
_____ Ottawa vice ring
__X__ appearance on Front Page Challenge

_____ Montreal and Toronto airports closed
The minister refers to applicant as
_____ You (4 points)
_____ Whatsis (3 points)
__X__ My oldest and dearest friend (no point)

Hockey players only
Defecting from _California_ (If Czech National team, 10 points)
Nickname (Big Ned, Big Red, etc.)
Ricky Dick
Method of defection preferred, if to be arranged by scouts _____ Taxi _____ Hay wagon _____ Orient Express __X__ Other
Salary required in first year:
_____ $50,000 (2 points)
_____ 150,000 (6 points)
__X__ 200,000 (9 points)
Has Alan Eagleson ever run his hands over your body?
_____ Yes __X__ No (For reference only)

Criminal activities
He is **not** a crook.
He says.

Writers and artists only
Has most of your writing been done in:
__X__ U.S. (10 points)
_____ Britain (10 points)
_____ Chile (minus 50)
_____ All others (0)
_____ Canada (Canadian writers and artists should be discouraged from re-entering the country.)
Have you ever applied for/received a Canada Council grant?
__X__ Yes _____ No (If no, why not? See if applicant fails General Knowledge Sequence.)

Settler's effects
Please check the goods you intend to enter Canada with:
__X__ Money (10 points)
__X__ Furniture (4 points)
__X__ Money (10 points)
__X__ Colour TV (3 points)
__X__ Money (15 points)
__X__ Car (5 points)
__X__ Money (20 points)
__X__ More Money (50 points)

General information
Applicants should display a definitive knowledge of Canada before entry as proof they are familiar with Canadian customs (and are not too stupid to apply to the Canada Council).
Answer the following:
Where is Niagara Falls?
__X__ Kingston (9 points)
_____ Squamish (2 points)
_____ St. Boniface (4 points)
Why does a chicken cross the road? (To get to the other side, 8 points; all other answers, (10 points.)

Inspector's assessment
Richard is developing skills in remedial reading class and is an active participant in class projects and Show and Tell. He might work harder at social interaction and weaving.
H. Hardy.
H. Hardy, RCAF (Ret.)

ADMITTED.

IT IS HELPFUL TO THE APPLICANT TO HAVE FRIENDS AND BUSINESS ASSOCIATES IN CANADA TO ASSIST HIM IN SETTLING. WHICH OF THE FOLLOWING ARE FRIENDS OR BUSINESS ASSOCIATES?
_____ Lucien Rivard _____ Friendly Giant _____ Mitchell Sharp _____ Juliette _____ Harold Ballard _____ Jack Webster

▮✦ Immigration Canada

PORT OF ENTRY INTERVIEW FORM FOR POTENTIAL LANDED IMMIGRANT

Warning: DO NOT SHOW THIS FORM TO APPLICANT OR THE GLOBE AND MAIL
BY ORDER OF THE MINISTER

POINT TOTAL MUST EQUAL AT LEAST 60 OF POSSIBLE 100 FOR ENTRY.

Yellow peril

__Dr. Robert Fong__   __4/6/76__   __H. Hardy__

Name of applicant	Date **Name of Interviewing Officer**
(no points for knowing name)	(25 points for knowing name)

National Origin
Orangeman (10 points)
United States (10 points)
Europeans (except Wops) (8 points)
Wops (2 points, 3½ if hard worker)
Chinks (no points, unless railroad under con-
struction)
Polacks (1 point; 15 if agree in writing to settle in
Newfoundland)
Pakistani, West Indian and other riffraff (are you
kidding?)

Appearance of applicant
_____ Trendy (10 points)
_____ Jeans (minus 10)
_____ Boutique jeans w/appliqué (7 points)
_____ Busines suit and external affairs briefcase
(20 points)
_____ John Turner hairsyle or other Dry Look
(5 points)
_____ Gay (minus 2)
_____ Racist lecturer (5 points)
__X__ *Yellow*

DO NOT WRITE IN THIS SPACE

Why the hell not?

Race, which we are not allowed to ask
The Canadian Government abides by all dictums of the Human Rights Act and would never think of asking the racial background of an applicant. Ha ha. What colour are you? _____ White (10 points) _____ Black (1 point for trying) _____ Red (none) _____ Albino (2) _____ Paisley Print ($3.99 a yard)

CHINK.

Friends of Minister
Met minister at
_____ party
_____ embassy function
_____ Ottawa vice ring
_____ appearance on Front Page Challenge

N.A.

_____ Montreal and Toronto airports closed
The minister refers to applicant as
_____ You (4 points)
_____ Whatsis (3 points)
_____ My oldest and dearest friend (no point)

Hockey players only
Defecting from __Hong Kong__ (If
Czech National team, 10 points)
Nickname (Big Ned, Big Red, etc.)
__Chink__
Method of defection preferred, if to be
arranged by scouts _____ Taxi
_____ Hay wagon __X__ Orient
Express _____ Other
Salary required in first year:
_____ $50,000 (2 points)
_____ 150,000 (6 points)
_____ 200,000 (9 points)
Has Alan Eagleson ever run his hands
over your body?
_____ Yes __X__ No (For reference
only)

Criminal activities
Ran for student council, 1952.

Writers and artists only
Has most of your writing been done in:
_____ U.S. (10 points)
_____ Britain (10 points)
_____ Chile (minus 50)
__X__ All others (0)
_____ Canada (Canadian writers and artists should be discouraged from re-entering the country.)
Have you ever applied for/received a Canada Council grant?
_____ Yes _____ No (If no, why not? See if applicant fails General Knowledge Sequence.)

Settler's effects
Please check the goods you intend to enter Canada with:
_____ Money (10 points)
_____ Furniture (4 points)
_____ Money (10 points)
_____ Colour TV (3 points)
_____ Money (15 points)
_____ Car (5 points)
_____ Money (20 points)
_____ More Money (50 points)

General information
Applicants should display a definitive knowledge of Canada before entry as proof they are familiar with Canadian customs (and are not too stupid to apply to the Canada Council.
Answer the following:
Where is Niagara Falls?
__X__ Kingston (9 points)
_____ Squamish (2 points)
_____ St. Boniface (4 points)
Why does a chicken cross the road? (To get to the other side, 8 points; all other answers, (10 points.)

REJECTED.

Inspector's assessment
Speaks with accent. Didn't know time of last night's final goal. Smiles too much. Inscrutable. __H. Hardy__

H. Hardy, RCAF (Ret.)

IT IS HELPFUL TO THE APPLICANT TO HAVE FRIENDS AND BUSINESS ASSOCIATES IN CANADA TO ASSIST HIM IN SETTLING.
WHICH OF THE FOLLOWING ARE FRIENDS OR BUSINESS ASSOCIATES?
_____ Lucien Rivard _____ Friendly Giant _____ Mitchell Sharp __X__ Juliette _____ Harold Ballard _____ Jack Webster

THE BOARDROOMS OF CANADA'S AD AGENCIES DON'T HAVE MANY WOMEN.

WHY NOT?

Policy decisions made in the boardrooms of Canada's advertising agencies had a tremendous influence on advertisements for International Ladies' Year. They affected their content, their style, their design, as well as the quality of their message. Yet most of the women you see in the boardrooms of Canada's advertising agencies are serving coffee to the men who made those decisions.

So why weren't more women involved in these advertisements at the boardroom level? Why weren't more women involved at middle and upper management levels? Are women so conditioned into believing that only men have ulcers and alcohol problems that they hesitate to climb the ladder of advertising success? Or is the ladder pulled out from under their feet if they take one step too many?

Perhaps the answer lies with us. The sexist male copywriters who write the ads for International Ladies' Year.

Being a male copywriter is a full career and a demanding one. Being a male copywriter means writing ads that patronize women. Ads about pink dishwashing liquids that leave hands lotion-mild soft. About all-temperature deter-

gents that wash husbands' shirts whiter than white. About lemon-flavoured furniture polishes that make dining-room tables shine newer than new.

It means writing ads that tell women that their place is in the home — washing dishes, cleaning the oven, polishing furniture, washing hubby's shirts and socks. Ads that make women feel strange and abnormal if they want to be bankers or brokers, carpenters or caretakers, printers or politicians.

In short, being a male copywriter means creating subliminal prejudicial barricades for women. Barricades that tell them their place is in the home, subordinate to their spouses.

The question is, why don't we stop? Why don't we refuse to write sexist ads like that? Why not?

Maybe we've all been conditioned into not caring enough. Maybe. But, if an advertisement, a commercial or a promotion discourages women from pursuing any career they choose, then we should try to change them. We should make our voices heard. We should talk to each other and to those whose influence we need. Account executives, senior vice-presidents, even the big corporations who hire us to write the ads.

And we should talk to the bigwigs on the boards of directors of advertising agencies. As equals. We should liberate ourselves from the oppressive, uncreative work we do. Why not!

If you'd like more information on male copywriters responsible for the status of ladies, all you have to do is write us or drop in on your nearest ad agency.

If you'd like a "Why Not!" button, and a set of posters, just mention it when you stop by.

We're here to squeeze as much money out of the government as we can.

WHY NOT!

NATIONALIST ENQUIRER

LARGEST CIRCULATION OF ANY CANADIAN NATIONALIST TABLOID

SCIENTISTS DISCOVER . . .

AMERICAN PAPERBACKS LINKED TO LUNG CANCER

Max Saltsman . . .

Canadian Nationalism Saved My Marriage

Adrienne Clarkson Tells Us . . .

Forget Paul Newman and Robert Redford. Elwood Glover is My Sex Symbol

Stephen Lewis . . .

The CIA is Out to Get Me

Scandal At The CBC . . .

Is Lloyd Robertson's Hair Dressing Manufactured In New York?

Eric Kierans Charges . . .

The English Nanny Racket. An Insidious Attempt To Retard the Canadianization of Our Infants

Mel Watkins Tells The Enquirer: I've Fallen In Love!

Man-about-nationalism Melville Watkins is floating on air these days. After taking a very private motor trip through the Maritimes, he reports he's fallen in love with that region all over again. (Exclusive interview on page 10.)

I Secretly Watched "Hawaii Five O" And "The Waltons" Until Laurent Picard Showed Me The Path To 100% Canadian Content

Watching confident, greying Walter Gordon sit back in his made-in-Canada leather chair, one would hardly guess this ardent champion of a Canadian-controlled economy once was addicted to American television.

"I can laugh about it now," chuckles the affable former Finance Minister, "but I can remember it was getting to be a real problem."

"It was getting so," chimes in his smiling wife, "that he wouldn't even switch to Lloyd Robertson and 'The National'. He wanted to see Ed McMahon on the Budweiser commercial that comes between 'Cannon' and 'Eyewitness News'."

Gordon grimaces as he remembers those painful times. Sneaking out of Cabinet meetings to watch "Let's Make A Deal". Coming late to evening business conferences because he wanted to see if Marcus Welby could save his terminal arthritis patient. Neglecting his job and family for "Bowling For Dollars", "Celebrity Billiards" and "The Dating Game."

"I couldn't stop," he confesses. "I tried cold turkey, listening only to Peter Gzowski and 'This Country In The Morning'. I watched Elwood Glover at lunch for 23 straight days. I even wrote away for an autographed picture of Tommy Hunter and The Rhythm Pals."

But is was all to no avail. Things got worse, not better.

"I couldn't give it up," Gordon recalls. "I couldn't start the day until I had watched 'Captain Kangaroo' or The CBS Morning News. I lived for the weekends when I could watch 'NFL Highlights' or 'Zoo Parade'. And the highlight of my week was seeing Morris The Cat on a Nine-Lives tuna commercial."

Gordon nearly breaks down in tears as he recalls this horrible chapter in an otherwise distinguished nationalist career.

"It was all one big nightmare," he adds, "until the day I watched Laurent Picard at a CRTC hearing."

The rest is public knowledge now. The bold, articulate Picard, dedicated to 'The National' and 'Singalong Jubilee', forcefully selling the virtues of 100 percent Canadian content.

"Picard pointed out the merits of 'Take Thirty' and 'Reach For The Top', recalls a now smiling Walter Gordon. "It was his example that inspired me to watch 'Viewpoint' and 'This Is The Law'. In fact, it wasn't long before I was switching channels from 'Rhoda' to 'The Irish Rovers'."

Walter Gordon believes he's cured now. It's been six months since he's watched Ed McMahon, seven months since he's seen Morris The Cat.

But there's a lesson here for all nationalists. CBC vigilance is the price of cultural autonomy.

Or as a happy Walter Gordon now put it, "Thank God for men of vision like Laurent Picard!"

Vancouver Teacher Adds Novel Decorating Touch

Vancouver history teacher Roberta Stelkins believes in practising what she preaches.

A member of the Committee For An Independent Canada and a staunch believer in Canadian nationalism, Roberta decided it was time to add a touch of the nationalist spirit to her home.

"I was always telling my students how important it was to think Canadian," she told the NATIONALIST ENQUIRER. "And one day the realization hit me, there was absolutely nothing distinctively Canadian about my apartment."

Once her nationalist consciousness was raised, however, Ms. Stelkins sprang into action.

Not only did she redo her apartment in authentic Confederation-era furniture, but she added some even more imaginative touches of early Canadiana.

In particular, Roberta had her self-cleaning oven removed, and in its place substituted an original 18th-century pioneer hearth.

In the space once occupied by her living room sofa, she built an authentic blacksmith's smithy. And as yet another touch of early Canadiana, she had her bathroom repapered in log veneer.

Finally, as the crowning touch, Roberta had the windows of her 45th floor apartment redone, complete with shutters and pre-Confederation masonry.

Pictured below, Roberta peeks out of the remodelled window of her 45th floor dining room, happy that she's been able to bring a touch of nationalism to apartment living.

NO LAUGHING MATTER

Noted Canadian authoress Margaret Atwood has often complained about the slow development of indigenous Canadian humour in this country, a problem she usually feels is no laughing matter. However, last month the picture momentarily brightened for Margaret when a CBC representative played her tapes of the radio program "Inside From The Outside". "It's the worst program I ever heard," she commented, "but for some reason I can't stop laughing. Do they really get paid to do that?"

History teacher Roberta Stelkins looks out from the completely remodelled window of her 45th floor apartment.

College Students Go Early Canadian

Dressing "Canadian" is the latest rage to hit Canada's campuses, always an early barometer of the national mood.

And if the University of Saskatchewan is any indication, then the country is in store for a new wave of nationalist expression in clothes and dress.

Pictured below are three members of the Regina chapter of Sigma Py Y, the only totally Canadian fraternity on the Regina campus.

Members have discarded the traditional college blue jeans for a more indigenously Canadian look. Complete with pioneer hat and coat, their new "Early Canadian" outfits are nothing less than a knockout, and the fellows report they've never been so popular with the gals.

Clothing stores in the campus area report a growing demand for the new "Early Canadian" look, and the fad is said to be spreading right across Canada.

So don't be surprised if you soon see spiffy television newscaster Lloyd Robertson sporting the "Early Canadian" look on the 11 o'clock news!

College kids sport the new "Early Canadian" look as they stop for a sandwich and soda at the campus malt shop.

BECOME MORE CANADIAN WHILE YOU SLEEP THROUGH CBC RADIO AND TELEVISION!

ASTONISHING BUT TRUE!

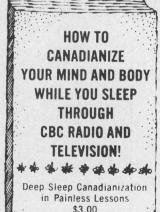

HOW TO CANADIANIZE YOUR MIND AND BODY WHILE YOU SLEEP THROUGH CBC RADIO AND TELEVISION!

✳ ✳ ✳ ✳ ✳ ✳ ✳ ✳

Deep Sleep Canadianization in Painless Lessons
$3.00
By Harry Boil

NOW YOU CAN:

- Develop a stronger Canadian consciousness
- Erase your unhealthy addiction to "Sixty Minutes" and "Kojak"
- Learn to watch National Film Board shorts without grimacing
- Control your desire to turn the channel while watching "Man Alive"
- Discover the secret of why Barbara Frum laughs at Larry Zolf and Patrick McFadden on "As It Happens"
- Learn to make real Canadian candy-floss in your bathtub, listening to "This Country In The Morning"

THE CANADIANIZED BROADCASTING CORPORATION

A Division of Bureaucrat Enterprises

BE MORE MILITANT *Instantly!*

Uplift Your SOCIALIST LIFE! WITH INVISIBLE "MILITANT" VOICE TAPES

Tired of being called wishy-washy? Slip a "militant" voice tape into your mouth anywhere. Then activate the hidden solenoid-operated control on your adam's apple. THE RESULT: A CHOICE OF SIXTEEN SELECTED SPEECHES ON ECONOMIC AND CULTURAL NATIONALISM, spoken by the leading proponents of the movement. You can select from: 1) "Canada's Dependent Status As A Resource Base And Consumer Market For The American Empire" by James Laxer 2) "Nationalism And The New Waffle" — Speeches From The October 1974 Council Meeting; and from many, many more selections, all in life-like stereo sound.

DON'T WAIT ANOTHER MOMENT! SEND IN TODAY!

Now you don't have to feel inferior and inarticulate. Gain new confidence and stature, as you denounce corporate American Imperialism, scream "sell-out" at the federally-assisted Syncrude project, denounce Mitchell Sharp as a tool of the BRASCAN robber barons. THESE LIGHTWEIGHT, EASY-TO-SWALLOW TAPES will not jam or break. Guaranteed for the life of your commitment to nationalist working class socialism. These tapes are designed to produce a LIFELIKE, STEREO sound. Your friends and colleagues will never guess it's the "militant" voice tape that's doing the talking. They'll envy your new confidence and militancy. BRIGHTEN UP WINE AND CHEESE PARTIES, win a full professorship, become chairman of your study group, take on the editorship of your journal. THOUSANDS OF NATIONALISTS have already taken advantage of this unbelievable offer.

Please state neck or collar size.

10 DAY TRIAL! Money Back Guarantee! Just send name, address and proof of Canadian citizenship. Pay postman on delivery only $320 plus postage for complete set of MILITANT NATIONALIST VOICE TAPES. Or send only $320 with order and we pay postage. 10 DAY TRIAL! MUST SATISFY OR RETURN AND MONEY WILL BE REFUNDED. Not responsible for law suits, loss of job, or visits from the R.C.M.P. as a result of contents of tapes.

THE MILITANT CO.
Dept. SELL-OUT
Nationalist Drive, Ottawa

NATIONALIST
ENQUIRER

100% Canadian Content

Prominent nationalists Abraham Rotstein, Peter C. Newman and Walter Gordon stop for a quick 100% Canadian content lunch at the newest "in" place for nationalists, Norm's Bar & Grill in Welland, Ontario. Special for the day was hot hamburger surprise with french fries and baked beans.

The Show Must Go On!

Stompin' Tom Connors has always been a real trouper, and last week when he sprained his left ankle on stage in Charlottetown, he continued that tradition. Although in extreme pain, he completed the show standing on only one foot through the entire performance.

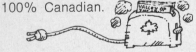

The Fred Davis Photo Album

FRED AT HOME   FRED ON THE JOB

FRED HAPPY   FRED SAD

FRED AWAKE   FRED ASLEEP

FRED SMILING

FRED SULKING

FRED AFTER LEARNING THAT TEAM
CANADA HAS BEATEN RUSSIANS 4-1

FRED AFTER LEARNING THE RUSSIANS
HAVE BEATEN TEAM CANADA 8-1

FRED READS THE MORNING SMILE

FRED SEES THIS PHOTO ALBUM AND RIPS
IT UP

More plain talk about phone bills. Golly yes.

Ours:

Item	1050 B.C. – 1975 A.D.
Electricity	up 8,020%
Cookies	up 10,000%
Postage	up 16,900%
Ice Skates	up 14,500%

Yours:

Item	1975 Jan. 1 – Jan. 3
Basic residence telephone service	up 1.5%

Good golly whillickers, folks. Who'd have thought it would come to this?

Don't your eyes hurt reading this teeny tiny type, hoping to find some explanation of why we're milking all you people out there in telephone land every month, or a hint of the exciting new flim flam we're taking to the Canadian Transport Commission for approval. (You remember the Canadian Transport Commission. They're the swell bunch of guys who approved our **last** rate increase, yesterday afternoon.)

Golly, don't your eyes hurt. This type is so damn small. Our market researchers tell us that only one out of every 2.5 million of you will still be reading at this time, and we don't intend to tell you a thing. So you might as well give up.

Besides, we've pretty well filled the space we wanted to, and that isn't easy when you've got nothing to say.

So just remember our corporate goal that promises "the highest possible profits at the highest possible price," and ask yourself . . . why didn't you protest to the Canadian Transport Commission when you could've?

After all, the rest of that corporate goal reads, "we want to make sure you get exactly what you deserve!"

FROM THE DESK OF

H. DAVID DIAL

VICE PRESIDENT OF
CREATIVE ACCOUNTING

MEMO:

RE: Classical Statistical Gibberish Ad

Dear Dave and Don:
Just a note to you boys down there in ad-land about your
recent masterpiece, comparing current costs to those in 1050
B.C. Should our new rate increase be approved, I think we
could compare costs back to 3,000 B.C. for an even more
striking comparison.

Could we go back to the Stone Age? Before copper was
invented or wherever the hell the stuff comes from? It
might be a good comparison statistic. You know how the
Canadian Transport Commission eats up those figures. I've
received many compliments on that recent 5,500-page brief
we dumped on them recently. The dummies opposing us at the
rate increase hearing can't even lift the bugger, not to
mention read it.

I've shipped out a copy of the brief and the ad to the
Centre for Creative Lying in New York — and I'm sure you
boys won't be forgotten when the big Awards Time rolls
around. Might even be good for an intro at the annual stock-
holders meeting to a couple of those little old ladies.
Ha ha.

I can't tell you how proud it makes me feel to see this
hype being created right here in Canada, rather than at our
New York agency. Remember what I've always said: Canada is
more than a country. It's a Branch Plant.

Again, a terrific job on that ad. Lord, I don't know how
you guys sleep at night.

Dave.

H. DAVID DIAL

HIST 382   **Revolution and Counter-revolution**   2L: MF2
               In Rosedale

An examination of the origins, course and outcome of the resettling of Toronto's prestigious Rosedale district by the nouveau riche. Among topics to be treated are militancy in the ranks of orthodontists, the eclipse of the Bay Street stock broker, and the economic roots of the cathedral ceiling. Students will be encouraged to examine a renovated townhouse first-hand.

HIST 383   **Canada in the Great Depression**   3T: WTS3
An examination of the Great Depression of 1975-76, including the energy crisis, spiralling inflation, unprecedented unemployment, increasing political corruption and the bankrupt leadership of the Liberal government. Discussion will centre around the topic which has intrigued historians for years: Why didn't anyone do anything about it?

CANADIAN AMERICAN SOCIOLOGY

Canadian American Sociology seeks an understanding of the determinants and patterns of Canadian social life, in terms of the determinants and patterns of social life in California and New York.

A uniquely Canadian discipline, Canadian American Sociology incorporates the most salient features of American Sociology and adds the proud and unique feature of teaching and applying this body of knowledge in Canada.

Canadian American Sociology covers the full range of sociologies studied in the United States, including even the study of American imperialism in developing nations. Of course, no mention is made of the imperialistic aspects of applying American sociological concepts to a uniquely Canadian context, since 78% of our faculty is American and they need the jobs.

Knowledge of Canadian American Sociology isn't good for much, but many of our graduates have been successful in obtaining jobs in some of the finest universities in Canada (teaching Canadian American Sociology to future Canadian American Sociology teachers). It must be noted, however, that in order to qualify for such positions, American citizenship, or three years' postgraduate work in the United States, is recommended.

More detailed descriptions of courses, together with full bibliographies, may be obtained by writing to any major Sociology department in the United States.

CAN AMER SOC 101 **Introduction to Canadian** 2L: MW1, 2T: MW1
American Sociology

An introduction to the basic principles and methods of Canadian American Sociology, with a focus on how to make research projects carried out in Minneapolis, Los Angeles and Detroit seem relevant to Canada. Plus an introduction to the methodology of advanced grant-getting and the theory of how to use big words that don't mean anything.

CAN AMER SOC 200 **History of Sociological** 3L: M1/M1:10/M1:20
Thought

A comprehensive look at the history of Sociological thought from the eighteenth century to the present, including a detailed study of prominent social theorists in France, Germany, Britain, Denmark, Norway, Sweden, Japan, Italy, Israel, Afghanistan and the United States. Additionally, if time permits, a minute and a half of lecture time will be devoted to the development of social thought in Canada.

CAN AMER SOC 201 **Race and Ethnic Relations** 1L: F2, 3T: F2

A study of race and ethnic relations in Canada, utilizing published studies of racial conflict in Harlem, social disorganization in San Francisco's Chinatown and ethnic mobility patterns in New York's East Side. Also a look at the structure of social relations in French Canada and the struggle, in the 1970's, between the Church and Premier Duplessis and his ruling Union Nationale Party.

Prerequisite: Taste for French, Chinese or Italian food

CAN AMER SOC 202 **Canadian Society** (Not offered 1970-1999)

Course content to be determined at a later date, if time, weather, faculty disposition, prevailing winds and the price of butter permit.

CAN AMER SOC 203   **Sociology of Economic**   5L: M9-5, T10-6, W9-5,
                    Development   Th3-8, F2-9

A structural-functional approach to economic development in resource-rich, under-industrialized nations. Examination of the benefits of multi-national corporations, international unions and free-trade agreements with fully-industrialized nations like the United States. Other topics include nationalism viewed as a reactionary response to modernization, and the dysfunctional role of foreign-investment controls in a free market economy.

Prerequisite: Year's subscription to Reader's Digest and Fortune Magazine

CAN AMER SOC 302   **The Horizontal Mosaic**   (Not offered
                    (Social Stratification in Canada)   1979-1986)

Empirical studies demonstrate that Canada's stratification system is not unlike the real one in the United States.

CAN AMER SOC 303   **Workshop in Applied**   1S: F6-6:15
                    Canadian American Sociology

An exploratory workshop in the utilization of American sociological concepts and research tools to win big government grants in Canada. Examples include transforming projects to resettle the endangered American long-horned elk into projects to resettle Canadian Eskimoes, and changing blueprints for the integration of Alabama schools into blueprints for the integration of the Canadian armed forces. Particular attention will be paid to refining sociological double-talk and learning to fill government research reports with hundreds of pages that don't mean anything.

Prerequisite: Not too much integrity.

CANADIAN ENGLISH LITERATURE
The study of Canadian English Literature seeks to stimulate the creative imagi-

Political Bubble Gum Cards

Trade you Two Real Caouettes for One Pierre Trudeau!

Cut them out and trade them with your friends...!

PROGRESSIVE CONSERVATIVE

ROBERT STANFIELD

LIBERAL

EUGENE WHELAN

2 ROBERT STANFIELD

LEADER OF OFFICIAL OPPOSITION   PROGRESSIVE CONSERVATIVE
Riding: Halifax   Political Style: None   Politically Leans:
                                                  Right-Centre
Born: 4-11-14   Birthplace: Truro, Nova Scotia
Nickname: Boring Bob   1st Parliamentary Session: 1967

OFFICIAL PRO COMPUTER PERFORMANCE RATING

STRONG POINT OF POLITICAL GAME	WEAKNESS OF POLITICAL GAME
Straight, honest, down-to-earth, non-spectacular approach to problems.	Straight, honest, down-to-earth, non-spectacular approach to problems.

BEST POLITICAL PITCH
Not to say anything.

FAVOURITE POLITICAL PLOY	REALLY MEANS
"I'm afraid I'll need more information before I can answer that question."	"I'm afraid I'll have to consult Dalton Camp before I answer that question."

SYNOPSIS
At times, shows great
promise, but can't
consistently deliver.
Strong leadership problem.
Early retirement expected.

ELECTORAL RECORD

	ELECTIONS	WINS	LOSSES	CABINET POSTS
FEDERAL	4	4	0	0
PROVINCIAL	6	6	0	2

29 EUGENE WHELAN

MINISTER OF AGRICULTURE   LIBERAL
Riding: Essex-Windsor   Political Style: Overwhelming
                                    Politically Leans: Right
Born: 7-11-24   Birthplace: Amherstburg, Ont.
Nickname: The Eggman   1st Parliamentary Session: 1962

OFFICIAL PRO COMPUTER PERFORMANCE RATING

STRONG POINT OF POLITICAL GAME	WEAKNESS OF POLITICAL GAME
Folksy give-'em-hell style.	Never knows what he's talking about.

BEST POLITICAL PITCH
Wearing rumpled suit
and telling rural
audiences, "I'm just
plain folks like you."

FAVOURITE POLITICAL PLOY	REALLY MEANS
Telling consumers, "You've never had it so good!"	Consumers have never been so badly represented in the Federal Cabinet.

SYNOPSIS
Real political threat
in rural areas. Career
somewhat slowed by mysterious
disappearance of 23,000,000 eggs.

ELECTORAL RECORD

	ELECTIONS	WINS	LOSSES	CABINET POSTS
FEDERAL	7	6	1	1
PROVINCIAL	0	0	0	0

NEW DEMOCRATIC PARTY

TOMMY DOUGLAS

LIBERAL

MITCHELL SHARP

14   TOMMY DOUGLAS

MEMBER OF PARLIAMENT   NEW DEMOCRATIC PARTY
Riding: Nanaimo-Cowichan-The Islands   Political Style:
        High Key   Politically Leans: Left
Born: 10-20-04   Birthplace: Falkirk, Scotland
Nickname: Terrible Tommy   1st Parliamentary Session: 1935

OFFICIAL PRO COMPUTER PERFORMANCE RATING

STRONG POINT OF
POLITICAL GAME
Good political orator.
Can go on for hours.

WEAKNESS OF
POLITICAL GAME
Who wants to listen to
any politician for more
than three minutes!?

BEST POLITICAL PITCH
"If you'll do what I ask,
I'll end this speech."

FAVOURITE POLITICAL PLOY
Pre-election prediction:
"This election will see
the N.D.P. emerge as a
power on the national scene."

REALLY MEANS
"If we can win 10
seats, we'll be lucky."

SYNOPSIS
Still one of the N.D.P.'s
big threats in the Commons.
Packs mean left jab that
still can hurt.

ELECTORAL RECORD

	ELECTIONS	WINS	LOSSES	CABINET POSTS
FEDERAL	10	7	3	0
PROVINCIAL	6	5	1	3

8   MITCHELL SHARP

PRESIDENT OF PRIVY COUNCIL   LIBERAL
Riding: Eglinton   Political Style: Wishy-washy
        Politically Leans: Right
Born: 5-11-11   Birthplace: Winnipeg, Man.
Nickname: The Apologist   1st Parliamentary Session: 1963

OFFICIAL PRO COMPUTER PERFORMANCE RATING

STRONG POINT OF
POLITICAL GAME
Great compromiser.
Can find a compromise
for anything.

WEAKNESS OF
POLITICAL GAME
Sometimes the solution
to a problem calls for
something other than
compromise —like
leadership.

BEST POLITICAL PITCH
"I agree with you
wholeheartedly."

FAVOURITE POLITICAL PLOY
Telling questioner,
"I'll take that
under advisement."

REALLY MEANS
"I won't answer that
question right now and
hope you'll forget you
ever asked it."

SYNOPSIS
Career on the skids.
Probable candidate for Senate

ELECTORAL RECORD

	ELECTIONS	WINS	LOSSES	CABINET POSTS
FEDERAL	5	4	1	4
PROVINCIAL	0	0	0	0

PROGRESSIVE CONSERVATIVE

JACK HORNER

NEW DEMOCRATIC PARTY

DAVID LEWIS

21 JACK HORNER

MEMBER OF PARLIAMENT   PROGRESSIVE CONSERVATIVE
Riding: Crowfoot   Political Style: Ornery
    Politically Leans: Far Right
Born: 7-20-27   Birthplace: Blaine Lake, Saskatchewan
Nickname: The Unilingual Kid   1st Parliamentary Session: 1958

OFFICIAL PRO COMPUTER PERFORMANCE RATING

STRONG POINT OF
POLITICAL GAME
Grass-roots links with
Diefenbaker Western
Conservatism.

WEAKNESS OF
POLITICAL GAME
Grass-roots links with
Diefenbaker Western
Conservatism.

BEST POLITICAL PITCH
Grass-roots links with
Diefenbaker Western
Conservatism.

FAVOURITE POLITICAL PLOY
Grass-roots links with
Diefenbaker Western
Conservatism.

REALLY MEANS
Grass-roots links with
Diefenbaker Western
Conservatism.

SYNOPSIS
Relies rather heavily on
grass-roots links with
Diefenbaker Western
Conservatism.

ELECTORAL RECORD

	ELECTIONS	WINS	LOSSES	CABINET POSTS
FEDERAL	7	7	0	0
PROVINCIAL	0	0	0	0

25 DAVID LEWIS

RETIRED   NEW DEMOCRATIC PARTY
Riding: (Formerly York South)   Political Style: Erudite
    Politically Leans: Left
Born: 6-23-09   Birthplace: Swislocz, Poland
Nickname: Dapper David   1st Parliamentary Session: 1962

OFFICIAL PRO COMPUTER PERFORMANCE RATING

STRONG POINT OF
POLITICAL GAME
Excellent politician. Whole
family steeped in politics.

WEAKNESS OF
POLITICAL GAME
Keeps losing elections

BEST POLITICAL PITCH
"Did I ever tell you the
one about the corporate
welfare bums?"

FAVOURITE POLITICAL PLOY
"If my party takes power,
I promise . . ."

REALLY MEANS
"There's as much chance
of my having to do what
I promise as Garfield
Weston voting N.D.P.!"

SYNOPSIS
Virtually retired now. But
still formidable opposition leader
under minority conditions.
Could make a comeback if
circumstances are right.

ELECTORAL RECORD

	ELECTIONS	WINS	LOSSES	CABINET POSTS
FEDERAL	10	4	6	0
PROVINCIAL	0	0	0	0

LIBERAL

JOHN TURNER

SOCIAL CREDIT

REAL CAOUETTE

30 JOHN TURNER

MINISTER OF FINANCE   LIBERAL
Riding: Ottawa-Carleton   Political Style: Beautiful
                               Politically Leans: Right
Born: 6-7-29   Birthplace: Richmond Surrey, England
Nickname: Robert Redford   1st Parliamentary Session: 1962

OFFICIAL PRO COMPUTER PERFORMANCE RATING

STRONG POINT OF   WEAKNESS OF
POLITICAL GAME   POLITICAL GAME
Dynamic, good looking,   a politician has to
aggressive, confident,   accomplish something to
appealing. Wow!   be elected Prime Minister

BEST POLITICAL PITCH
"Yes, I'll be free to speak
to the riding associations
Women's Club on Monday."

FAVOURITE POLITICAL PLOY   REALLY MEANS
Stare directly into T.V.   "If this doesn't work,
camera with baby-blue eyes. I'm really in trouble."

SYNOPSIS
Has qualities to be elected Liberal
captain. However, a bit too perfect.
Look for off-season switch to World
Bank.

ELECTORAL RECORD

	ELECTIONS	WINS	LOSSES	CABINET POSTS
FEDERAL	6	6	0	6
PROVINCIAL	0	0	0	0

5 REAL CAOUETTE

OPPOSITION LEADER   SOCIAL CREDIT
Riding: Témiscamingue   Political Style: Entertaining
                           Politically Leans: Right-Left
Born: 9-26-17   Birthplace: Amos, P.Q.
Nickname: Mr. Funny Money 1st Parliamentary Session: 1946

OFFICIAL PRO COMPUTER PERFORMANCE RATING

STRONG POINT OF   WEAKNESS OF
POLITICAL GAME   POLITICAL GAME
Charismatic. Great orator. Rarely makes sense.
Brings crowds to their feet.

BEST POLITICAL PITCH
"Print more money."

FAVOURITE POLITICAL PLOY   REALLY MEANS
"Print more money."   "Print more money."

SYNOPSIS
Often counted out, but
keeps coming back. Strong
rural support. Nice party
leader to have in Opposition,
but would make very strange
Prime Minister.

ELECTORAL RECORD

	ELECTIONS	WINS	LOSSES	CABINET POSTS
FEDERAL	10	7	3	0
PROVINCIAL	1	0	1	0

(POLITICAL AFFILIATION UNKNOWN)

GERDA MUNSINGER

NEW DEMOCRATIC PARTY

STANLEY KNOWLES

18   GERDA MUNSINGER

RETIRED   (POLITICAL AFFILIATION UNKNOWN)
Riding(s): (Not enough space to list)   Political Style: Intimate
                                    Politically Leans: (CENSORED)
Born: (Information Unknown)   Birthplace: East Germany
Nickname: (CENSORED)   1st Parliamentary Session:
                                    (Kept Work Outside of Parliament)

OFFICIAL PRO COMPUTER PERFORMANCE RATING

STRONG POINT OF   WEAKNESS OF
POLITICAL GAME   POLITICAL GAME
CENSORED   *CENSORED*

BEST POLITICAL PITCH
CENSORED

FAVOURITE POLITICAL PLOY   REALLY MEANS
CENSORED   *CENSORED*

SYNOPSIS
A judicial inquiry
in 1961 confirmed
that Gerda Munsinger
was a *CENSORED*

ELECTORAL RECORD

	ELECTIONS	WINS	LOSSES	CABINET POSTS
FEDERAL	0	0	0	2
PROVINCIAL	0	0	0	(UNKNOWN)

32   STANLEY KNOWLES

MEMBER OF PARLIAMENT   NEW DEMOCRATIC PARTY
Riding: Winnipeg North Centre   Political Style: Refreshing
                                    Politically Leans: Left
Born: 6-18-08   Birthplace: Los Angeles, California
Nickname: Zzzzzzzzz   1st Parliamentary Session: 1942

OFFICIAL PRO COMPUTER PERFORMANCE RATING

STRONG POINT OF   WEAKNESS OF
POLITICAL GAME   POLITICAL GAME
Veteran Parliamentarian.   Easy to fall asleep
Extremely knowledgeable.   to.

BEST POLITICAL PITCH
Opposed Parliamentary
pay raises.

FAVOURITE POLITICAL PLOY   REALLY MEANS
Refers to Parliamentary   Who knows? Outside of
rules of procedure.   Stanley Knowles, who in
                             Parliament ever paid any
                             attention to Parliamentary
                             rules of procedure?

SYNOPSIS
Great parliamentarian. Carries
astounding .916 winning election
average into House. Can be boring
zzzzzzzzzz

ELECTORAL RECORD

	ELECTIONS	WINS	LOSSES	CABINET POSTS
FEDERAL	12	11	1	0
PROVINCIAL	0	0	0	0

PROGRESSIVE CONSERVATIVE

GEORGE HEES

LIBERAL

PIERRE TRUDEAU

---

13   GEORGE HEES

MEMBER OF PARLIAMENT	PROGRESSIVE CONSERVATIVE
Riding: Prince Edward-Hastings	Political Style: Excessive
	Politically Leans: Right
Born: 6-17-10	Birthplace: Toronto, Ont.
Nickname: Gorgeous George	1st Parliamentary Session: 1950

OFFICIAL PRO COMPUTER PERFORMANCE RATING

STRONG POINT OF
POLITICAL GAME
Extremely charming.
Very photogenic.

WEAKNESS OF
POLITICAL GAME
You can't charm away
unemployment and
inflation.

BEST POLITICAL PITCH
"Would you like to
take my picture?"

FAVOURITE POLITICAL PLOY
"Which would you prefer,
full profile or a direct
head and shoulders
shot?"

REALLY MEANS
"I should've kept
that job as President
of the Montreal Stock
Exchange."

SYNOPSIS
Still has strong
following. Smile still
bright as ever. Look
for one last run for leadership
of Conservative team.

ELECTORAL RECORD

	ELECTIONS	WINS	LOSSES	CABINET POSTS
FEDERAL	10	9	1	2
PROVINCIAL	0	0	0	0

---

1   PIERRE TRUDEAU

PRIME MINISTER	LIBERAL
Riding: Mount Royal	Political Style: Varies
	Politically Leans: Left-Right-Centre
Born: 10-18-19	Birthplace: Montreal, P.Q.
Nickname: Le Roi	1st Parliamentary Session: 1965

OFFICIAL PRO COMPUTER PERFORMANCE RATING

STRONG POINT OF
POLITICAL GAME
Little alternative
for the voters.

WEAKNESS OF
POLITICAL GAME
See statistics on
unemployment, inflation,
balance of payments,
national debt and
foreign control of
economy.

BEST POLITICAL PITCH
"You never had it so good."

FAVOURITE POLITICAL PLOY
"You never had it so good."

REALLY MEANS
"Let them eat cake."

SYNOPSIS
Underwhelms opposition. Excellent
at taking vacations during periods
of crisis. Extensive four-letter
vocabulary. Sure bet in 1978
and 1982.

ELECTORAL RECORD

	ELECTIONS	WINS	LOSSES	CABINET POSTS
FEDERAL	4	4	0	2
PROVINCIAL	0	0	0	0

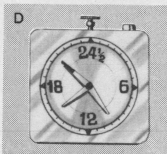
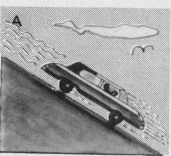

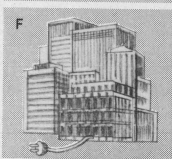

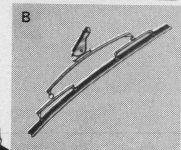
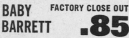

December 6, 1977

Dear Pensioner,

It is with regret that I must inform
you that, because of rising costs, the Department of National
Health and Welfare can no longer continue its home convalescent
care programme for the elderly.

Beginning January 10th, payments for
supplementary home medical care for the elderly will no
longer be available from this department.

I know the curtailment of this subsidy
will cause much hardship among needy segments of the
over-sixty population, but the funds for such a programme
are simply not available.

In this regard, I refer you to the ad
on this subject currently running in your local newspaper
and in Time and Maclean's magazines.

As the ad points out, the cost of
subsidizing the home convalescent plan has risen by
$2,000,000 in the last two years, additional funds for
which we simply don't have. Hence the need to phase out
the programme in the coming year.

Again, my apologies for any hardship
the curtailment of this much-needed programme may cause
you. I assure you there was no other choice.

Yours sincerely,

John McFadden

John McFadden
Asst. Deputy Minister

GRANT, NORVATH, WARWICK & CO.
MANAGEMENT CONSULTANTS
RIDLEY BUILDING
14 METCALFE ST.
OTTAWA, ONTARIO

June 29, 1977

PRIVATE

Mr. John McFadden
Asst. Deputy Minister
Dept. of National Health and Welfare
Ottawa

Dear Mr. McFadden:

Re: Home Convalescent Plan For The Elderly

After two years of careful study, we are pleased
to submit the enclosed report on the projected costs of contin-
uing your department's home convalescent plan for the elderly.

It is our basic finding that your cost projections
two years ago were correct and that the cost of maintaining
the plan will increase by the exact amount (two million
dollars) you predicted.

Please find our final bill for this work, allocated
according to the following distribution of staff time, fees
and overhead:

1. Research Design	$50,000
2. Research Implementation	$275,000
3. Computer Time	$50,000
4. Printing & Other Costs	$35,000
	$410,000

Thanking you in advance.

Yours sincerely,

Heywood Grant,
Senior Partner

INTERNAL MEMO - NOTE DE SERVICE

Subject / Objet : <u>ADDITIONAL FUNDS FOR HOME CONVALESCENT</u>
<u>CARE PROGRAMME</u>

FROM / DE:

Charles Linson
Budget Co-ordinator
Special Accounts
Treasury Board

TO / À:

John McFadden
Asst. Deputy
Minister
Dept. of Health
and Welfare

Looks like you'll have to consider
scrapping the home convalescent care
programme.

The two million dollars I had hoped to
scrape up for you from Manpower's cash
overflow will have to go into cost of
living bonuses for Members of Parliament.

As you probably recall, salary increases
for M.P.'s were pegged to the consumer
index when they voted themselves that
second 33% increase in November 1976.
And now with inflation running at a
36% rate, I'll be lucky if I don't end
up in the red.

Sorry, but that's how the special accounts
cookie crumbles.

Chuck

Charles Linson

CL/jc
July 16, 1977

July 28, 1977

Dear John,

    Here's the information you asked for, in case the matter's brought up in the House.

    The audit isn't finished yet, but Walter feels it's going to cost at least $600,000 to wind down the Home Convalescent Programme.

    Sounds like a lot, but it's not that much when you consider we have to buy our way out of thirty different 25-year leases on executive offices right across the country. Not to mention getting only 50¢ on the dollar for all that expensive telex equipment.

    Why the hell Leslie had to have all the offices broadloomed is also beyond me. It must have cost at least $25 a square yard. And while we're on the subject, what the hell are we gonna do with all those five hundred dollar paintings he rented? It

PROPOSED SEVERANCE PAY OFFERS
HOME CONVALESCENCE PLAN STAFF

AUG 19, 1977

NAME	POSITION	Number of Years Contract Runs	ANNUAL SALARY	SEVERANCE OFFER	GO AS HIGH AS	COMMENTS
Bill Walters	Executive Assistant	5	$35,000	$800	$15,000	Hard-nosed bugger. Go easy.
Leslie Hanson	Executive Assistant Assistant	8	$33,000	$300	$20,000	Not very bright. Might settle for a thousand.
Herb Millen	Regional Manager	5	$40,000	$2,500	$35,000	A thief. He's already stolen us blind. It'll be worth $35,000 to be rid of him.
Martin Ball	Public Relations	6	$30,000	$50	$100	Has terrible self-image. Play on his guilt.
Rita Sorenson	Information Officer (CLASS ONE)	3	$25,000	$400	$10,000	Tell her she's looking great. Take to dinner.
Sonya White	Information Officer (CLASS TWO)	3	$24,975	$2,000	$19,000	Women's lib. Watch out. She reads the papers.

PROJECTED TOTAL SEVERANCE PAYMENTS $375,000.

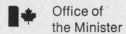

Office of the Minister

Department of National Health & Welfare

October 16, 1977

Dear John,

About that $170,000 in public relations money that idiot Macgregor didn't spend when he managed the home convalescent care plan in 1969. Lucky our auditors stumbled on it before Treasury got wind of it. They'd have spent it by now.

I'd appreciate it if you could funnel the bulk of the money (about $165,000) into the Local Initiatives Programme. In particular, Northumberland Riding looks weak right now, and if we could give them the money they want for their damn Pancake Week, I think we could buy

Internal Memo/Note de service

Date December 21, 1977

Subject/Objet PUBLICITY EXPENSES RE: CURTAILMENT
OF HOME CONVALESCENT CARE PLAN

From/De Bill Walters
Executive Assistant

To/À

John McFadden
Asst. Deputy
Minister

John,

As requested, here's the final breakdown of
expenses for publicizing the winding down of
the home convalescent care plan for pensioners:

Local Newspaper Ads	$85,000
Maclean's Inserts	$35,000
Time Inserts	$45,000
Press Luncheon	$25,000
Smith, Foster, Lewis Advertising Agency	$175,000
	$365,000

Hope you got your free bottle of booze from the
press luncheon. My regards to Mary.

Sincerely,

Bill

Bill Walters

BW/cm

Jan. 6, 1978

John,

Funniest thing. For a joke, Sue in the
accounts department added up all the expen-
ditures of our department in closing down
the home convalescent care program for
pensioners.

You'll never guess what the final total
was. Two million dollars!

Don't believe it? Add up the figures
yourself:

Consulting Fees	$410,000
Liquidating Offices & Equipment	$600,000
Severance Pay	$375,000
Settling Printing Account	$85,000
Balancing 1969 Accounts	$165,000
Publicity	$365,000

$ 2,000,000

Well, I guess none of us is perfect.

By the way, that idea for a cartoon
series on traffic safety was a dandy. I'd
like to get the whole department working on it as

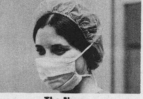
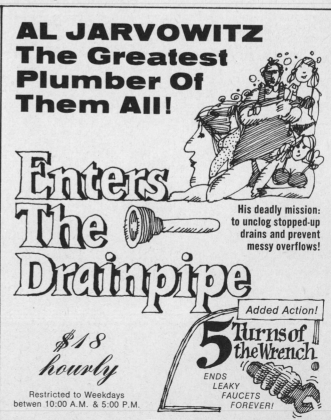

of the Future

BECOME A BULLY!

BEND MEN TO YOUR WILL!

Once I was like *you* — a nittering Nerd Niceguy, accommodating and serene.

Then I discovered The Secrets of Dynamic Tension — the scientifically-proven Isometric principles, cursing and shouting, that do away with the need for Conventional Politesse.

I started putting on weight.

My muscles developed.

My mouth got filthy.

Now I have a rippling, massive Majority Government; I command attention and homage; I crush those who oppose me like bugs with scorn, humiliation and outrage.

The press adores me. The masochists fall over each other in their rush to absorb my spleen.

When are you going to stand up for yourself?

Begin pushing people around?

Give back what you've been getting?

Say all those swell dirty words you've only been thinking for so long?

Write to me today: learn to do a forward somersault off a diving board . . . a Baby Bear Bounce on the Trampoline . . . how to have Children on Christmas . . . all my secrets revealed!

Don't delay!

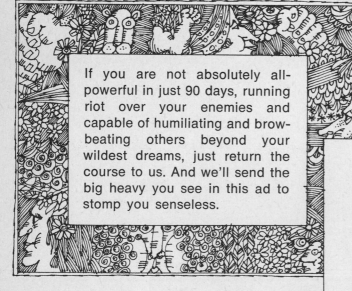

If you are not absolutely all-powerful in just 90 days, running riot over your enemies and capable of humiliating and brow-beating others beyond your wildest dreams, just return the course to us. And we'll send the big heavy you see in this ad to stomp you senseless.

Yes, rush my PT-101 COURSE in plain sealed wrapper! No salesman will call!

NAME_____

ADDRESS_____

CITY_____

PROVINCE _____ CODE_____

☐ Check here if non-English-speaking Frog.

MONEY BACK IF NOT FULLY SATISFIED!

Internal Memo/Note de service

Date March 12, 1978

Subject/Objet NEW BLOCKBUSTER CBC-TV DRAMA SERIES

From/De Ernest Featherbedding, Head, TV Drama

To/À

Whoever's CBC
President When This
Memo Reaches Him

Please find attached material on TV Drama's newest
blockbuster series, The National Turkey.

We here in TV Drama feel certain we have <u>at last</u> come up
with <u>the</u> formula that will bring us true success, i.e.,
sales to the BBC, ITV, Granada, ABC, NBC, CBS, NATO, SEATO,
or <u>somebody</u> outside of Canada.

Granted, we have made occasional misjudgements in the past
about the success of our more expensive series. Granted.
Nevertheless, we feel the attached material on our upcoming
project proves beyond any doubt that we have truly <u>learned</u>
<u>from our failures in the past</u>.

On the following page, you will find a scene from the first
episode of the proposed series, introducing the leading
characters. On the page following it, you'll find a brief
plot synopsis of the episode, along with a schematic chart
indicating the leading characters by name, as they appear
in that scene.

We're very excited about The National Turkey here in TV
Drama, and once you've read the enclosed materials, I think
you will be too.

Nos morituri te salutamus.

E.F.

Ernest Featherbedding

Canadian   Société
Broadcasting   Radio-
Corporation   Canada

CBC 82 Bil. 12/74

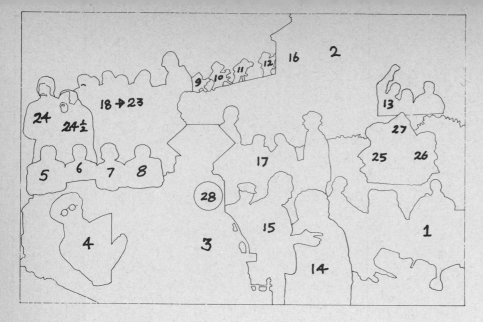

SYNOPSIS: EPISODE 1

The white folks (1) of Jalna (2), having resisted myriad attempts over the ages to deprive them of their ancestral home, face their greatest challenge ever as The National Nightmare (3) comes puffing and wheezing through their front yard, accompanied by various hangers-on (4, 5-8) and social climbers (9-12).

Rennie (13), in the meantime, has taken a part-time job as a researcher on a LIP project, studying the failure of TV drama in Canada in the 1970's.

Poor Adeline (14) has been driving the ancestral Edsel while under the influence, but fortunately she has been apprehended by none other than Wojeck (15) who is demanding that she explain why such a good series as his went off the air.

To pay the cost of repainting the mansion (2) white (16) every two weeks, the family has been forced to rent the west half of the front porch to Delilah (17); but since there is not much chance of her attracting a lot of business, the Beachcombers (18-23)

wait patiently to ransack this heirloom when the C.M.H.C. finally does forclose, while two mysterious strangers (24, 24½) leer over their shoulders.

Meanwhile, Radisson (25) and Groseilliers (26), having schlepped their canoe (27) through the bush for longer than any of us can remember, finally arrive in this WASP haven, and decide to pack it in permanently, leaving the historical field to the ghost of Paul Muni.

And speaking of survivors, has anyone noticed who's (28) taking a subtle look at the prospects of a comeback? We're not saying exactly who he is, but it's not Foster Hewitt.

Finally, the episode ends when the first audience ratings come in, and it's discovered that "The Uncle Bobby Show" has received double the audience on that other network.

Nevertheless, undaunted, the series continues to bad reviews, ultimately justifying its title as "The National Turkey!"

POLLUTION SUPERSTARS

MULTI-NATIONAL CORPORATE SPORTS ILLUSTRATED

EXCLUSIVE:
THE PRESIDENT OF INCO
RATES THE TOP TEN
INDUSTRIAL POLLUTERS

SPECIAL:
SCOUTING REPORTS ON
200 EXECUTIVE
VICE-PRESIDENTS

EXCLUSIVE FEATURE
COMPLETE ONTARIO & QUEBEC
PRICE-GOUGING STATS
FOR '75-'76

OFFICIAL STANDINGS:
WORLD-WIDE STRIP-MINING
COMPETITON

PHOTO FEATURE:
CANADA'S TOP TWENTY
BRANCH PLANTS

I. T. & T.
After Chile...What Next?

HOWARD HUGHES
My Ten Favorite Cartels

CORPORATE FANS SOUND OFF

PLANNED OBSOLESCENCE

Sirs:

I read your article "Ten Ways To Cheat The Consumer" (August '75) with much interest. However, I think your writer overstates the value of the hidden monthly interest charge.

In my experience as a vice-president of a small children's toy company, I've found planned obsolescence is the real path to a higher yield and bigger profits. Naturally, there is the slight risk of negligence suits in the case of a swing or slide collapsing and injuring the children playing on it; but that's what we have good lawyers for, isn't it?

MARTIN MALLOW
Montreal, P.Q.

COMPUTER TELLS ALL

Sirs:

Congratulations on Walter Lacey's September feature story on the new WCR computer.

Amassing information on the private sex life of credit card holders is a stroke of genius. Just let them try and get behind in their monthly payments, and out comes the appropriate file, complete with names, dates and places.

A little friendly hint that the information might end up with the newspapers, or fall into the hands of the little lady at home, and presto, the monthly statement is quickly paid.

Now how about an article on the use of Mafia strong-arm tactics to collect unpaid telephone or utility bills?

M. FRANK
Mississauga, Ont.

JUST DESSERTS

Sirs:

I am a long-time fan of the Voyageur Arms Company.

For years now, this small Canadian company has been quietly manufacturing small arms for the American Army without any public recognition. Yet their pistols have been worn by American officers in Viet Nam, Cambodia and the Dominican Republic.

They've even been instrumental in the success of anti-Communist coups in Chile, Greece and Guatamela.

Isn't it time this company received the public recogniton other companies like Dow Chemical and the Lougheed Corporation have already received?

JIM FRIGHT
Edmonton, Alta.

DRAM CHEMICAL: 1, OPPOSITION: 0

Sirs:

Hurrah for the Dram Chemical Corporation! It's about time someone spoke out against anti-pollution controls (July '75).

What we need is more proponents of an unfettered free-enterprise system. After all, if the residents of Deer Lake choose to breathe, it's their problem if they develop lung cancer from asbestos particles leaked into the air by the Dram plant.

Thank goodness there are still outspoken executives like Dram President William Smirk. Let's have more articles on big business standing up to the Socialist hordes!

ROBERT PARTICLE
Victoria, B.C.

INCREASED WORK LOAD

Sirs:

How about more coverage for the neglected sport of exploiting secretaries?

I suggest a series on the eight best ways to coax an increased work load out of a secretary without raising her salary.

My nomination for the best method goes to the tried-and-true art of flattery, telling your girl Friday how well she looks, or complimenting her on her new pant suit.

For me, it works every time.

LARRY NEXUS
Halifax, N.S.

From The Corporate Wire

It's a hat trick for Dynamic Industries' Walter "Winkie" Williams. Walter has been appointed Chairman of the Board of Dynamic Industries Of Canada Ltd.

Previously he was Chairman of the Board of Dynamic Industries of Peru Ltd. and Dynamic Industries of Dar es Salaam Ltd. before both those companies were nationalized by their respective host governments.

Walter isn't expecting any problem in Canada though, and expects Dynamic to continue its policy of shipping copper and zinc back to the United States to be manufactured into electrical parts and components.

"I expect to be here a long time," he told a press conference in Toronto. "The Canadian government is known for its very generous policy in these matters."

*　　*　　*

The Mavis-Irvin Pharmaceutical Company plans to announce a proposed settlement of a suit against the Company by unhappy users of its nasal decongestant, NASEL-MIST. As reported in The Financial Post, several thousand users have suffered such varied side effects as blindness, paralysis and kidney failure after using NASEL-MIST Spray.

Until recently, Mavis-Irvin has maintained that all the above-mentioned side effects were listed in ⅛-inch print on the side of NASEL-MIST atomizers. The company insisted that if the complainants had taken the time to read this information with a magnifying glass, they would have been sufficiently warned.

Now the company has softened its position; and although it still won't acknowledge responsibility for the unwanted side effects, it acknowledges that the complainants didn't receive adequate relief of their sinus congestion or stuffed-up noses.

As compensation, Mavis-Irvin is offering $1.29 to each complainant to buy a rival decongestant spray.

*　　*　　*

"We're number one, we're number one!" That was the chant of shareholders at the annual meeting of the Magatino Spaghetti Company. In fact, Magatino's is also number two, three, four and five, since it bought out its last competitor, the Italian Noodle Company, last month.

In the last three years, the Magatino Company has managed to gain control of every phase of the spaghetti business by buying out all competition at the manufacturing, packaging and retail ends of the business. In the words of the company president, "a clean sweep."

The company has announced that the price of packaged spaghetti will go up three dollars next week because of "rising costs."

*　　*　　*

The Melchen Construction Conglomerate has completed negotiations with the Energy Ministry of South Yemen to build the country's first hydroelectric dam.

Although South Yemen doesn't have any rivers or waterfalls, Melchen officials have convinced the Ministry to go ahead with the dam to boost South Yemen's declining world prestige.

The Minister of Energy personally announced the terms of the agreement from his new $300,000 yacht, and invited reporters to a reception at his new $800,000 home in Switzerland, where he announced plans to retire next year.

*　　*　　*

1976-77
North-American Pollution Preview

Here's how the pollution race should end up after the 1977 winter season . . .

AIR POLLUTION

UNITED STATES
1. Macme Chemical Corp.
2. Stamford Steel Co.
3. Strenco Industries

CANADA
1. Macme Chemical Corp. (Canada) Ltd.
2. Stamford Steel Co. (Canadian Division)
3. Strenco Industries of Canada

WATER POLLUTION

UNITED STATES
1. Meriden Lead Ltd.
2. Oxide Chemicals
3. Multiple Aluminum Co.

CANADA
1. Meriden Lead (Canada) Ltd.
2. Oxide Chemicals of Canada
3. Multiple Aluminum Co. (Canada Division)

MWP AWARD (MOST WASTEFUL POLLUTER)
Arcom Plastics

MOST CHILDREN POISONED
Rampat Lead Co.

MOST WILDLIFE DESTROYED
Universal Oil & Exploration Limited

MOST WORKERS PREMATURELY RETIRED
Lamburt Asbestos Limited

NEWS-MAKERS

Friendly Persuasion

When it comes to foreign aid the United States is understandably gun-shy about repeating its mistakes in South-East Asia. The State Department is now a little more careful about who gets all those American greenbacks, but when a nation qualifies, Washington will still pull out all the stops to make it feel appreciated. Witness the latest infusion of aid into Luxemburg, where before a national television audience, American Ambassador Richard Lham handed over $35,000,000 in cash to appreciative Luxemburg Prime Minister, Hans Bejiford. Following Bejiford's instructions, the money was in small bills of varied denominations. He was last seen boarding a plane to Switzerland.

Message From Workers

Things have been slow in the construction industry lately, and angry workers have been looking for an appropriate way to express their discontent. When a spokesman for the Labour Department stopped to call at union headquarters, members felt they had finally found a way to get their message across. Looking on are representatives of The Ontario Committee on the Status of Women who are protesting sexism in the minimum wage laws.

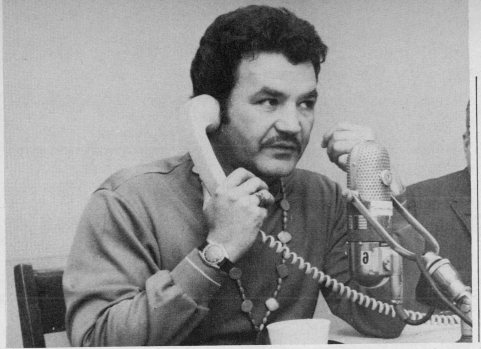

In Good Voice

For several seasons, actor Bruno Gerussi was the star of his own CBC Radio talk show and doting fans became accustomed to hearing his voice through the magic of the radio microphone. Now that he's left radio to star in the popular television series, ''The Beachcombers'', he must answer his telephone calls minus the microphone, and disappointed friends and colleagues complain he doesn't sound the same. Always ready to oblige, Bruno installed a microphone on his kitchen table and now insists on talking through it when answering telephone calls.

Players Strike Back

The NHL Players' Association has been trying to get a bigger slice of TV revenues for several seasons now. Finally, last week, when owners turned down their demands for the fifth time, players retaliated. In a game between the Boston Bruins and the Montreal Canadiens, players kept their backs to the television cameras for the entire game. Pictured is the winning goal by the Montreal forward line of Pete Mahovlich, Henri Richard and Guy Lafleur, as they skate in backwards on the sprawling Boston netminder.

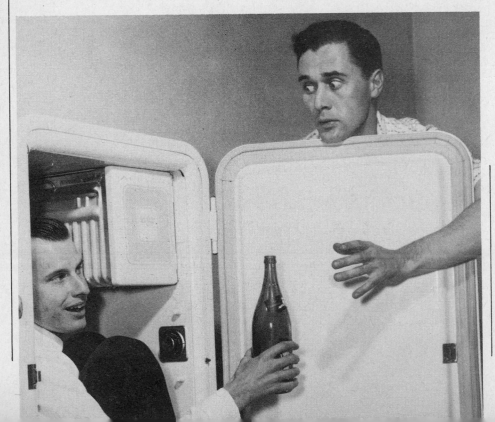

Optional Equipment

When Robert Watson of Regina bought his new Amano refrigerator with an automatic soft drink dispenser, he never dreamed the dispenser would be Amano Vice-President Tom Archer. Amano has been having problems with its regular mechanical dispensers, and has been toying with the idea of hiring welfare recipients on an hourly basis to dispense soft drinks from its refrigerators.

The Canadian Film Development Corporation, Argus Films and Pierre Berton proudly present

THE KIDNAPPING OF CHARLES TEMPLETON

You've Read the Book Heard the Record... Seen the T.V. Show!
NOW A MIGHTY MOTION PICTURE BLAZES TO THE SCREEN!!!

Based on the real-life kidnapping of famed Canadian author, broadcaster, evangelist, inventor, panelist, debater, newsman, reporter, commentator, writer, essayist & editor, Charles Templeton!

STARRING:

Blossom Rappaporte as Gerald Ford ★ Murray Westgate as Charles Templeton ★ Nina Lani Epstein as Flora Macdonald ★ Farley Mowat as Jack McClelland ★ Tommy Hunter as Dalton Camp ★ The Rhythm Pals as The Canadian Army ★ Al Cherney as Eugene Whelan ★ Leon Mangoff as The Pope ★

THE PRE-MEDS COLOURING BOOK

An Illustrated Primer
For Aspiring Young Physicians

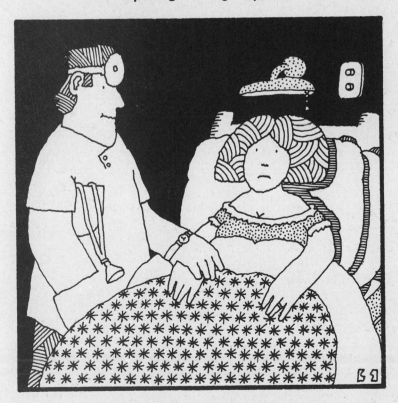

Published by GREED BOOKS
A Division of Impersonal Industries Ltd.
21 Medical Square
Vancouver, B.C.

doctor
This is the doctor.
He is dedicated to helping the suffering.
He is dedicated to healing the sick.
He is also dedicated to making a lot of money.
Colour him green, especially his wallet.

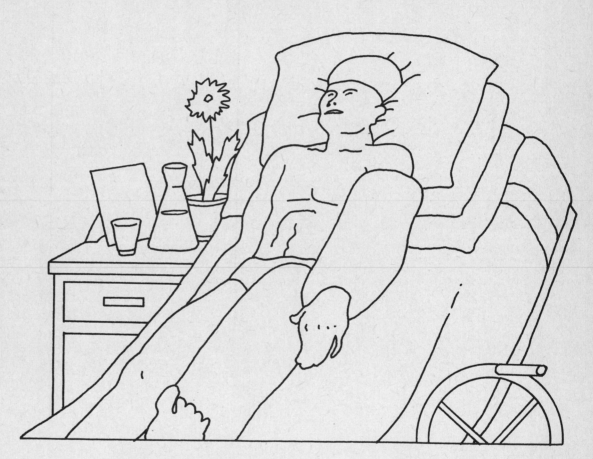

patient
This is the patient.
The patient is sick.
Wait till the doctor tells him
he doesn't make housecalls.
He'll be even sicker.
The doctor then bills his Health Insurance
for a telephone consultation.
Colour the patient green.

health insurance

This is government-sponsored
Health Insurance.
It is socialized medicine.
It is bad for doctors.
It is a menace to patients.
It is ... Who are we kidding?
It's terrific!
Colour it green. Very green.

ONTARIO HEALTH INSURANCE PLAN

IDENTIFICATION CARD / CARTE D'IDENTITÉ

| 12 | 73 | MCLACHLAN | B3 | 21009241 | 31 |

office

This is the doctor's office.
Notice the waiting patients.
Notice they've been waiting three hours.
Notice how the doctor doesn't apologize
for keeping them waiting three hours.
After all, when else can a doctor call his stockbroker?
Colour the doctor's office green, especially
if Alcan Aluminum goes up 15 points.

answering service

This is the answering service.
"I'm sorry the doctor is busy right now."
"I'm sorry the doctor cannot be reached right now."
"I'm sorry the doctor is not taking any calls right now."
Uncle Henry is breathing his last breath.
The answering service won't get the doctor.
Colour Uncle Henry a palish blue.

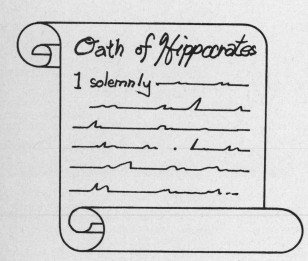

hippocratic oath

This is the Hippocratic Oath.
What is it?
Who knows?
Who cares?
It doesn't have a cash-surrender value.
Don't even bother to colour it.

foreign doctor

This is a foreign doctor.
The foreign doctor comes from
funny places like India.
Funny places where they eat curry
and don't understand the value of money.
In other words, the foreign doctor works cheap.
Draw a quota against the foreign doctor
immediately.
Colour him black or brown.

hospital

This is the hospital.
It is a bold and noble experiment in healing.
It is the last refuge for the sick and dying.
It is also the only place where a doctor can see twenty-two patients in one visit
Colour the hospital green. Very, very green.

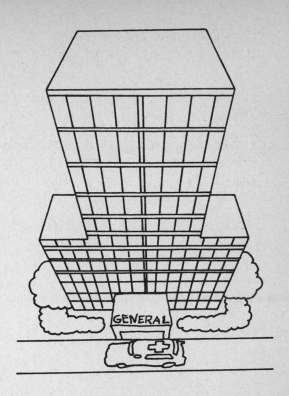

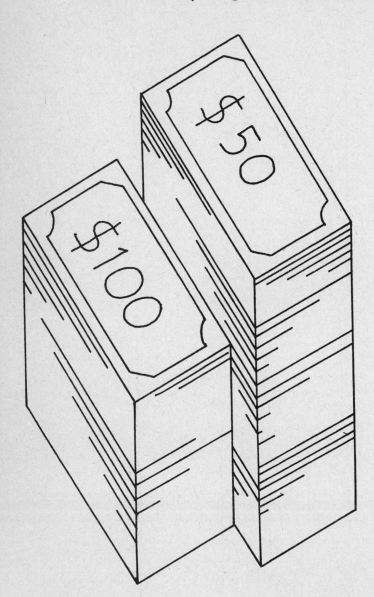

cash

This is cash.
Nice green cash.
So perfectly green you don't have to colour it.
Just grab it and run.
After all, isn't that what today's medicine is all about?

ARE <u>YOU</u> OLD ENOUGH TO JOIN THE CANADIAN SENATE?

Are you ready to make Big Money in your Declining Years as so many others do?
Then take this simple self-test in the privacy of your Home or Hospital.
Are you ready to sleep away the lazy days of summer at $450 a day?
Ready to eat duck à l'orange in the Parliamentary restaurant for $2.85?
Ready to spend the rest of your life babbling for Hansard?
Ready to fall asleep right now?
HEY! WAKE UP! TAKE THE TEST!

1. The prostate is
   _____ President of Argentina
   _____ Head of the Anglican Church
   _____ the opposite of negastate
   _____ like the hully gully.

2. Serutan spelled backwards is _____.

3. Which one of the following turns you on?
   _____ Anita Bryant
   _____ Ma Murray
   _____ Hot milk and honey grahams

4. If God had wanted us to have Good Government in Canada, he would never have given us
   _____ Grits
   _____ Tories
   _____ the CBC
   _____ the Rideau Club

5. Indians should go back to Africa, where they came from.
   _____ Agree
   _____ Disagree

6. Things could get worse.
   _____ Yes
   _____ No
   _____ Impossible!

7. Hardening of the arteries is
   _____ Hard
   _____ Easy

8. Is everyone you know dead?
   _____ Yes
   _____ No
   _____ Wish they were

9. I believe in
   _____ William Lyon McKenzie
   _____ Royal Canadian Legion
   _____ the Orange Lodge
   _____ Loblaws
   _____ the Joy of Sex

If you had the strength and presence of mind to answer five or more of the above questions, or check six or more boxes, then you're obviously not old enough to join the Canadian Senate. Tough luck. You're missing out on a good thing.

If you were unable to stay awake to answer five questions, or check six boxes, then you're obviously well-qualified for a Senate career. To find out more about an exciting appointment to the Canadian Senate, write to: Political Payoffs, Patronage Building, 31 Partisan Drive, Ottawa. There's nothing like a Senate appointment to pick up a flagging career!

TEN DAYS THAT SHOOK PARLIAMENT HILL!

ANOTHER IFTO EXCLUSIVE:

SCENES FROM THE EXCITING FILM THAT HAS SET OFFICIAL OTTAWA ABUZZ

"An eloquent response to those ten shameful days . . . a film you won't quickly forget."
— Martin Knelman, Globe & Mail

"A damning indictment that will sear the conscience of Canadians for years to come. . . A masterpiece of cinematic suspense."
— John Hofsess, Maclean's

(1) As the film opens Jean, Pierre and Gerard — close boyhood friends — are lunching together — oblivious of the gathering storm that threatens to engulf all of them.

(2) Meanwhile, in the tranquil capital city, life continues as usual, as the beautiful people meet to share in the day's gossip.

(3) Little do any of the protagonists in this real-life drama know of the terrible ordeal that awaits them and their nation.

(4) Then it happens. As Pierre talks with a visitor from the South, a passerby tells him the horrendous news: The price of a meal in the Commons Cafeteria has soared to twenty-eight cents!

(5) Pierre is shaken. Despite the calming words of his Southern visitor, he knows what this could mean. The business of the nation could grind to a halt, the country could be brought to its knees. The nation's legislators must have the sustenance they need, or a legislative famine could envelop the whole country.

(6) Pierre rushes to the Cafeteria, where he finds the diners are already in a panic. When he offers to sell his cup of coffee for seven cents, he is overwhelmed by the panicking populace, all begging him for this last chance to drink a really cheap cup of coffee.

(7) Soon word of the Cafeteria price increases spreads through the city and the panicked population tries to use every available means of transporation to leave the doomed metropolis. They know that without a decent meal for their legislators and civil servants, the only result can be a sinking ship of state.

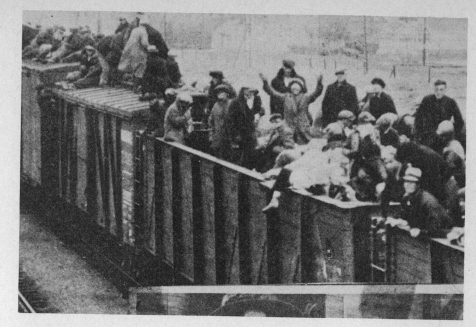

(8) Panic has spread everywhere and the police and army can no longer keep order. Pierre takes to the streets, trying to calm the frightened populace. "You've never had it so good," he shouts at the desperate throng, and slowly they respond to his calming message.

(9) Pierre returns to a deserted Hill only to find that the panicking Cafeteria diners have set it afire. Tirelessly, he works with a few loyal aides to quell the blaze, and then returns exhausted to his office to decide on a plan of action.

(10) Meanwhile, the leader of the opposition clique on Parliament Hill has not been idle. In a secret basement hideaway, he plans his strategy for taking control of the panicked city.

(11) Even more ominous is the presence of the mastermind of so many nefarious deeds in the halls of Parliament. The mysterious magician of backroom strategy tells all who will listen that he's just in Ottawa to see the tulip festival.

(12) Pierre knows time is against him. Already the armies of Separatism are marching on the Eastern borders of the city. He must find a way to restore the cheap meals in the Commons Cafeteria and right the sinking ship of state.

(13) Pierre confers with his closest aides. They work out a plan. The future of the nation rests on their shoulders.

(14) Boldly Pierre confronts the leader of the opposition in a tense meeting. Unsure, the opposition leader challenges him to a duel — Commons branding irons at twelve feet.

(15) Pierre stands his ground, and finally the opposition leader reconsiders. He realizes he has been foolish in demanding voluntary or mandatory restraints by those around him. There must be another solution.

(16) The opposition leader smiles as Pierre tells him his plan. There'll be no need for branding irons now. Pierre has hit upon a foolproof plan.

(17) That night, at an impromptu banquet for the survivors on Parliament Hill, Pierre slowly rises to his feet. Then before the astounded throng, he announces his solution: raise the salaries of Members of Parliament by at least 33%. To a legislator earning thirty-five or forty thousand dollars a year, a 28¢ meal in the Commons Cafeteria would now seem cheap!

(18) Later a beaming Pierre receives the congratulations and thanks of a relieved citizenry. Order and good government would now reign once more. But no one who had lived through this trying week of crises would ever forget those ten days that shook Parliament Hill!

MealMakers.

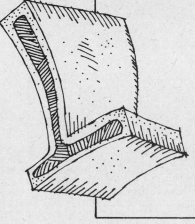

Cross Cut Shoe Leather Roast
SPECIAL!

$24.50 LB

T-Bone Steaks
MEATLESS SPECIAL!

$16.00 LB

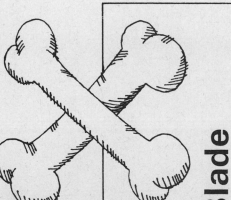

Frozen Stewing Pigeons
UNEVISCERATED SPECIAL!

$22.00 LB

Blade Roast Bone
FROM THE CHUCK, MARROW IN SPECIAL!

$5.00 LB

Doiminion

REDMATH BRAND
SUGAR
½ OZ. CUBE $2.50

ZIPPY
OLD FOLKS' SPECIAL
DOG FOOD
8 OZ. TIN $3.98

RICHERMELLO SPECIAL 16 OZ. PIE
DANDELION PIE
$1.98

SPOILED PINK
GRAPEFRUIT
10 FOR $8.80

SPOILED IN FLORIDA.
SIZE 48'S   SPECIAL!

HIGHERLINER, FROZEN
CATFISH FILLETS
LB. $1.80

MINUTE-LADY, ORANGE FLAVOURED
FROZEN CONCENTRATED   8 OZ. TIN
CARROT JUICE
$1.90

BOREDOM   12 OZ. CARTON
2% MILK 98% WATER
$1.50

RICHERMELLO   10 OZ. BOTTLE
INSTANT WATER
$7.95

JUST LIKE REAL NOODLES!
WAGU CARDBOARD
SPAGHETTI
14½ OZ. PKG. $1.45

MARY WILES
WIENER SKINS
1 LB. PKG. $3.20

RIND ON, END CUT
OR CENTRE CUT
BREAKFAST BACON
A PIECE $6.95

FAST RELIEF FROM
HUNGER PAINS
BOYER STARVPRIN
BTL. OF 200 TABLETS $3.50

ALPIN BRAND, FROZEN
OWL MEAT PATTIES
1 LB. BOX $7.98

BLUEBIRD ARTIFICIALLY
COLOURED AND FLAVOURED
IMITATION
SOFT MARGARINE
1 LB. TUB $2.25

HERBERT'S PURE
CANADA FANCY
TURNIP JUICE
48 FL. OZ. TIN $2.25

CANARNATION
FRESH, IMITATION
SPINACH
8 OZ. PKG. $1.75

RICHERMELLO
CHEESE SLICE
CANADIAN PROCESS
1 OZ. SLICE $1.25   SPECIAL!

SWISS AROMA
SANDWICH BAGS
WAGGIES, PLASTIC   PKG. OF ONE $8.05   SPECIAL!

ASS'D VARIETIES
SUPPER MIX
CRAFT CARROT SURPRISE
8 OZ. PKG. $1.49   SPECIAL!

PLIPTONS, MIX
PIGEON NOODLE SOUP
4 OZ. PKG. $2.98

French
Fried
Potato
Peelings
32 OZ. PKG. $2.50

VALLEY MARSH
FROZEN
CRINKLE CUT
CANADA
CHOICE   SPECIAL!

RICHERMELLO
INSTANT COFFEE
½ OZ. JAR $10.89

GARDEN FRESH
GREEN BEANS
EACH $1.19   SPECIAL!

FROZEN EVISCERATED
CANADA GRADE "A"
TURKEY BONES
LB. $5.50

BICKLE BRAND
PICKLED GRAPE SEEDS
24 FL. OZ. BTL. $1.05

RICHERMELLO
ORANGE CHIFFON CUPCAKE
3 OZ. PKG. $1.35   SPECIAL!

BEEF, LAMB, PORK
MEAT FLAVOUR CRYSTALS
3.25 OZ. PKG. $1.85

LARGE SIZE
CANADA GRADE "A"
EGGS
$1.85 EACH

MEATY
BUDGIE BIRD RIBS
LB. $2.89   SPECIAL!

Joan Feedem Tells How:

Many of our customers have written in asking, "With inflation running at 51% how can the consumer make ends meet?"

The answer is outlined in my simple, easy-to-read, free booklet, "Twenty-one Ways To Fight Inflation." Actually, the booklet used to be free; but as I outlined in a previous column, rising costs forced us to add a 50¢ handling fee last June.

Unfortunately, escalating printing costs necessitated an additional 45¢ hike in September and 85¢ in January. Now you can still get your very own free booklet on how to fight inflation, but at a slightly higher price of $2.50. Just write to me care of:

"Rising Costs," Box 350, Ottawa, Ontario.

It's time we all pitched in to do our part in fighting the menace of inflation.

YOU SHOULDN'T HAVE ASKED US

WHAT GOES IN A HOT DOG?

HOW THE MISSILE RACE IS SHAPING UP

Could you please tell me about little-known Canadian explorer Henry Quinden? I've seen references to him in history books, but never the full story of his life.
Brian Footlocker, Owen Sound, Ont.

Not much is known about Henry Quinden's life, except that he was the illegitimate child of a convicted rapist, and was born in the backroom of a saloon in what is now Chatham, Ont., in 1832. From what we can gather from court records and newspaper accounts of the day, Quinden was violent and mean-tempered from the day he was born. At the age of three, he assaulted his mother with the butt of his musket, knocking out four of her teeth and fracturing her jaw. At age six, he became embroiled in a schoolyard fracas over a game of hoops, and stabbed a young kindergarten girl who sided with his opponents. Finally, at the age of ten, he was expelled from the local mission school after he threatend to kill the Jesuit schoolmaster for insisting that two plus two didn't equal five.
After leaving school, Quinden spent most of his remaining life in stockades and prisons. In the course of 15 short years, he was arrested for, among other things, theft, arson, aggravated assault, man-

slaughter and attempted murder.
In the duration, he married six times, fathering 23 children, all of whom he abandoned. During these short periods of freedom he also killed 18 people, most of whom, he insisted, looked at him "the wrong way."
On his 25th birthday, while trying to escape capture by the Mounties, Quinden made the discovery that has earned him a place in the annals of Canadian exploration. After ambushing a party of Mounties pursuing him, and shooting them in the back, Quinden fled into the Northern Ontario bush, travelling several hundred miles until he arrived at a hitherto undiscovered body of water, which he characteristicaly labeled Death Lake.
It was at Death Lake that Quinden was finally apprehended and shot. But the lake is better known as the site of one of the largest copper finds in Northern Ontario. Unfortunately, because of the inaccessibility and roughness of the bush country

HENRY QUINDEN

that surrounds Death Lake, no working mine has ever been established there, though more than $33,000,000, and the lives of 15 workers, have been expended in the effort. A fitting tribute to one of Canada's most mean-tempered explorers.

My girlfriend and I are having an argument. She says a normal store-bought hot dog or wiener is all beef. I say it can also contain pork or soy filler. Can you tell me who is right?
Pat Weatherspot, Agincourt, Ont.

Neither of you is right. Our experts tell us that a normal hot dog wiener contains meat by-products, wood shavings, dirt, saw dust, ecoli bacteria and rodent droppings. What's more, unless the hot dog is boiled at a temperature of 212 degrees Fahrenheit for six hours, salmonella poisoning can result. In addition, in 60% of the population, a slow case of cancer of the intestine can develop, though this can be avoided by drinking 42 ounces of distilled water after consuming your hot dog.

Whatever the case, to you and your girl friend, good eating!

How come the famous second line of the Cleveland Pats Allen Cup trophy winners was known as the "Beat" line?
Walter Muskoxen, Winnipeg.

Because all four members of the 1948-49 Allan Cup champions had been arrested, at one time or another, for wife-beating. Left-winger Charlie Fornisen held the team record in this category, having been arrested twice in 1944, three times in 1945, and on two occasions in 1946, '47, '48 and '49. (In 1950, he was divorced.) The other three members of the line were not as conspicuous, having been arrested for wife-beating only seven times during their stay with the team. However, right-winger Eddie Litzwork was later arrested on a charge of pedophilia after retiring in 1951.

Is it true that Soviet missiles launched against the United States could hypothetically be intercepted over Canadian air space?
Bruce B. Morrison, Lachine, Que.

Yes, it's true. In fact, the Pentagon plans anticipate intercepting 95% of all nuclear missiles aimed at the United States before they reach the American border. This means that most missiles aimed at the United States would be intercepted and destroyed over Canadian territory, with the ensuing nuclear explosion laying waste to 69% of our agricultural lands, destroying 76% of our major urban centres and killing half the population of our country. The other half, even if they lived, would be exposed to murderous radiation which could result in deteriorating health and a life-expectancy of seven-and-a-half months.

Do you have a question for which even your encyclopedia won't give you an honest answer? Do you have a feeling you are not being told the full facts about things? Want to really feel depressed about the world? Write to: You Shouldn't Have Asked Us, 201 Harbourgate Drive, Blahs, Ont. Sorry, but the volume of mail makes it impossible to send you a personally depressing reply.

THE DEPARTMENT OF INDIAN AFFAIRS "BIG WAMPUM" CATALOGUE

Spring and Summer 1881

Hundreds of exciting goods and services from your neighbourhood Indian Affairs agent at bargain prices!

Your chance to trade in a used lake or valley — a worthless forest or waterfall — for a bargain bonanza of government gifts!

A New Service Of The Department Of Indian Affairs
Through Its Network Of Local Indian Affairs Representatives

A MESSAGE FROM THE DEPUTY MINISTER OF INDIAN AFFAIRS

For too long our native peoples have been exploited and abused in their dealings with traders, merchants and settlers.

Now it is the purpose of the federal government, through its Indian Affairs Department, to offer the Indian people a fair and equitable settlement for any further lands or bodies of water they choose to barter.

Beginning with this catalogue, the Indian people need no longer fear being deceived or cheated by unethical traders or land agents. They can now bargain in good faith with their government, confident in the knowledge that they can trade their most worthless possessions — bothersome rivers, hard-to-manage forest acreage — for valuable gifts.

I know our Indian friends will be pleased with the wide selection of merchandise, services and special offers they'll find in this month's catalogue. In the coming months, we hope to increase that selection even more.

So sit back and browse through the following gift-packed pages of bargains, and enjoy, enjoy, enjoy!

R. M. McPherson

R. M. McPherson
Deputy Minister

BEAUTIFUL, MODERN SUBURBAN BUNGALOWS

All the conveniences of suburban living are yours in these spacious two-bedroom bungalows, situated on the rolling hills of the federal government's latest suburban development for Indians, Wanahee Reservation and Recreation Club. Special exclusive membership for Indians only. Protected status. Private police force and special schools. For your safety and security, "no drinking" laws.

No. 1213, Suburban Model Bungalows. . . . (Price) 15,000 acres of virgin forest land or mineral rights to 300 square miles of northern bush.

HIGHRISE LIVING IN THE HEART OF THE CITY

If city living is your choice, here's your opportunity to trade the harsh, subsistence existence of hunting and fishing in the country for untold opportunities to earn big money in one of Canada's thriving big cities. Gaze out over this urban wonderland from the balcony of your luxurious sixth-floor apartment,

LIGHT INDUSTRY BRINGS AFFLUENCE & IMPROVEMENTS TO TRIBAL LANDS

Now your tribe or band council can share in the fabulous profits of industrialization. For a small investment — a 150-year free lease, free materials and guaranteed cheap labour — you can have a lumber mill, scrap metal plant or aluminum smelter operate on your tribal lands. Of course, it will take at least 250 years before your people will be sufficiently qualified to have a say in management, and wages will have to be sub-standard to compensate for the poor location, and there will be some damage to fish and wildlife, but think of the prestige of having your own local industry. Not to mention such other benefits of industrial life as time clocks, canned goods and your own Brewer's Retail Store.

No. 3012. Light Industry. . . . (Price) Minimum 150-year free lease for use of tribal lands, including rights in perpetuity to all natural resources, plus guaranteed labour at 35¢ an hour.

as you plan a life of affluence and prosperity beyond your wildest dreams.

Now you can trade the dull day-to-day routine of hunting and fishing for the freedom and excitement of city life. Tavern and liquor store nearby. Unemployment insurance soon to be available.

No. 1411. Highrise Apartment In The City. . . . (Price) 2 medium-sized lakes or rivers, plus hunting rights to surrounding countryside.

TRAVEL OPPORTUNITIES

Tired of the cold northern climate? Looking for a change of scenery? Want to see something more exciting than a sunset or the Northern Lights? Then trade in your tribal hunting grounds — with all their messy oil and copper deposits — for an opportunity to travel and see the real world. You'll travel by rail to all the exciting fun spots of North America, including Sault Ste. Marie, Moose Jaw, Minneapolis and Duluth. You'll see life as it was really meant to be lived. An experience you won't want to miss. Meals, lodging and bail money not included.

No. 4321. Travel Opportunities. . . . (Price) Rights to 25,000 square miles of territory.

THREE ROOMS OF FURNITURE

Now's your chance to have the bedroom set and living-room and dining-room furniture you've always dreamed of. During the spring and summer seasons only, the government is once again offering these beautiful three-room ensembles **free** to the first three hundred tenants of its new Squamish Reservation housing complex. Factory-made and beautifully finished, this furniture will satisfy the tastes of the most discriminating buyer. Ten pieces in all. Includes eight-day guarantee.

No. 2314. Three Rooms Of Furniture. . . . (Price) Sign 25-year lease in government housing complex. Tear down old living quarters and sign over lands to the government.

MODERN AGRICULTURE REAPS HIGH PROFITS

Hunting and fishing were an acceptable endeavour many years ago, before the Indian learned the benefits of civilization. But let's be honest. How many rifles or axes will a venison steak buy? Or a day's catch of lake trout? Not many. What the truly modern Indian has learned is that the really high profit yields are in agriculture. Mechanized agriculture, on carefully-selected government lands, is your ticket to higher profits and a better life. Contact your local Indian Affairs agent and ask him to tell you about the advantages of giving up your unsettled nomadic life for the security of farming on specially-selected government lands. Exclusive tracts for Indians. Government supervision.

No. 1165. Modern Agriculture On Government Lands. . . . (Price) Relocation from present home site and forfeiture of all rights to such lands.

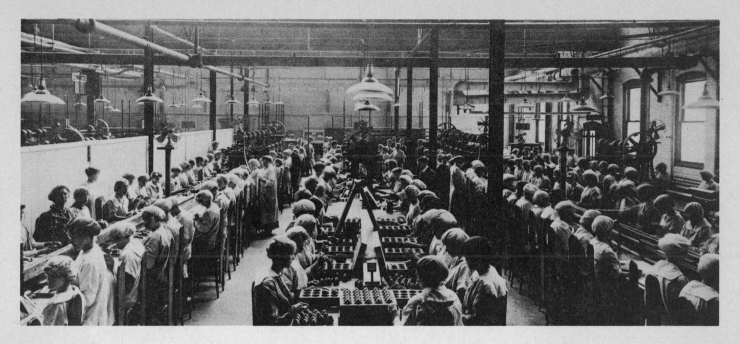

LEARN NEW TRADE

There once was a time when there was a need for such out-moded skills as wood carving, sewing one's own clothes, stalking deer. In today's modern industrialized world, however, the emphasis is on real skills, such as weaving cotton on mechanized factory looms and cutting patterns on the assembly line. And from now until February, the Indian Affairs Department, in conjunction with local industry, is willing to pay you two dollars a week to learn these skills as an apprentice in the textile mill of your choice. That's right, we'll pay you to learn a trade which could eventually earn you as much as eleven dollars a week. No education needed. Seven days of work a week guaranteed. Just stop in at your local Indian Affairs branch office for more information.

No. 5313. Apprentice On-The-Job Training. . . . (Price) Probably your health and sanity.

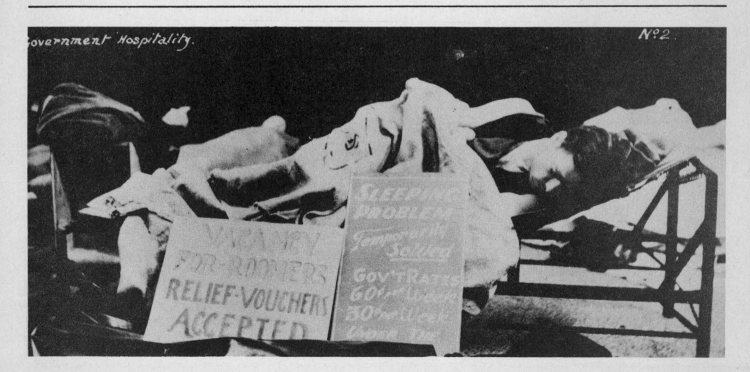

GUARANTEED SOCIAL SECURITY

As many keen social observers have noted, the price of progress is social and economic instability. A job available one year may not be available the next. Wild game that once flourished may suddenly become scarce. Rivers and streams that were once the source of much-needed fresh water may be diverted by industry, or polluted by industrial waste. The old way rapidly gives way to the new. How, then, can the Indian guarantee the security of himself and his family? Through a host of new medical, social and financial services offered by your neighbourhood Indian Affairs representative. The Indian Affairs Department is now prepared to offer every Canadian Indian social security from the day he is born to the day he dies, and at a modest price: his autonomy. Think about it.

No. 1819. Guaranteed Social Security. . . . (Price) Independence.

2 RECORD SET

Don'tel
TC-201

**BOB STANFIELD
& THE BANANAS**

**THE NOVA SCOTIA
PUBLIC OWNERSHIP
BLUES BAND**

ORIGINAL POLITICIANS
ORIGINAL HALF-TRUTHS

20 GREAT
POLITICAL HITS

P. E. TRUDEAU

EUGENE WHELAN

**JEAN MARCHAND
AND THE POLITICAL
PORKBARREL
BAND**

**JOHN TURNER
& THE REVENUE
DEPARTMENT
SINGERS**

STEREO
(can also be played on mono)

2 RECORD SET

Ⓓ
Don'tel
TC-201

Record One
Side One

1. *Where Have All The 23,000,000 Eggs Gone (Who Knows?)* . . . Eugene Whelan (1974)
2. *Unemployment Insurance Benefits To Remember* . . . Bryce Mackasey & The Billions (1973)
3. *Give My Regards To Dalton* . . . Bob Stanfield & The Bananas (1971)
4. *Hats Off To Harry (Hayes)* . . . The Western Establishment (1968)
5. *Put Your Cash In My Slush Fund* . . . Anonymous Quebec Cabinet Minister (1970, 71, 72, 73, 74, 75, 76 . . . . .)

Record One
Side Two

1. *The Best Things In Life Are Expensive* . . . The Inflation Singers (1975)
2. *Leaving On a Jet Plane – To Tel Aviv* . . . Marc Lalonde (1974)
3. *Asbestos Dust Gets In Your Lungs* . . . The Environment Protection No-Voice Chorus (1975)
5. *Help!* . . . Robert Bourassa (1975)

Record Two
Side One

1. *Jeepers, Creepers Where'd You Get Those O.F.Y. Grants* . . . Gerard Pelletier & The Sponges (1972)
2. *Fly Me To The Moon Or Anywhere Else The R.C.M.P. Can't Get Me* . . . Hal Banks (1966)
3. *Tears On My T-4 Forms* . . . John Turner & The Revenue Department Singers (Re-release)
4. *Crying In The Heavy Water Plant* . . . Nova Scotia Public Ownership Blues Band (1973)
5. *Four Strong Filibusters* . . . The Pipeline Debate 25 Voice Chorale (1956)

Record Two
Side Two

1. *Put Another Half-Billion In (Oil, Oil, Oil!)* . . . The Syncrude Serenade (1976)
2. *L.I.P. Grants Keep Falling On My Riding Association* . . . Jean Marchand & The Political Porkbarrel Band (1973)
3. *When Harold Cardinal's Smiling* . . . Jean Chretien (Still To Be Released)
4. *Happy Days Aren't Here Again* . . . P. E. Trudeau & Co. (1969, 1970, 1971, 1972, 1973, 1974, 1975, 1976 . . .)
5. *What's The Use Of Voting* . . . The Canadian People's Lament (Re-release)

DISTRIBUTED BY DON'TEL INTERNATIONAL LTD:

177 SIDE ST.
SASKATOON, CANADA

5555 RIPPLE DR.
HALIFAX, CANADA

PRODUCED IN ASSOCIATION WITH:

BANKRUPT POLITICS
OF CANADA LTD